PUBLISHING
& associates

MANY SONS UNTO GLORY

Lifestyle of an Overcomer

Steven Paul Sluder

bush
PUBLISHING
& associates

MANY SONS UNTO GLORY

ISBN: 978-1-944566-41-8 Print
ISBN: 978-1-944566-40-1 eBook

PUBLISHING
& associates

DEDICATION

To Dad and Mom. Thank you for putting the seed of the incorruptible Word of God in me as a child.

To Rejeanna and Ben. For standing in faith, not giving up, and laughing at the devil. He truly is a liar.

To Pastors Qwest and Lauren Gatlin for being my spiritual covering on this project. God knew I would need it. I love all of you.

CONTENT

FOREWORD

I want to begin this forward by stating "loud and clear"... that Jesus is the answer. You cannot meet Jesus and stay the same. He meets you right where you are, and before you know it, you begin to transform from the inside out. Similar to the example of the New Testament disciples, Steven's story is a shining example of a life inevitably transformed by the power of the Gospel of Jesus Christ and the presence of the Holy Spirit. It's that simple. Get around Jesus and your life changes... for the better!

If there is one thing I've experienced in my personal walk with God, and have also been witness to in the lives of others, it is that the enemy will do anything he can to distract and/or completely derail your walk with God (John 10:10, 1 Peter 5:8-9). We've seen Satan do this over and over again in scripture. He was even dumb enough to try and persuade Jesus to shift His worship from God... to Satan himself. We read in Luke 4:1–13 that Satan eventually left Jesus alone after failing to persuade Jesus of anything other than what He knew was TRUTH. Jesus would counter everything Satan said with this powerful statement, "It is written...". Even Jesus knew the power of God's written Word to thwart the devil's lies. I believe with all my heart, that God is raising up a generation of world changers who will combat the lies of the enemy with the written and spoken Word of God. Steven has done a brilliant job pairing personal testimony with biblical insights and Truths, that will absolutely change the lives of so many.

As a Pastor, there's nothing more powerful than being able to share the gospel and pair it with an authentic, honest testimony, like

Steven's. That is one of the many things that excited me about this long-overdue ministry tool. I believe that every 5-fold minister will find this book to be an incredible resource for your personal life and ministry as you continue to equip the saints for a life of ministry (Ephesians 4:11-12). I've personally learned to never underestimate the power of a great testimony, as we read in Revelation 12:11. I want to advocate for Steven, and this excellent book, which I know will assist in the rescue of others trapped in a life of sin, as well as assist ministers as a wonderful resource for reaching the lost, and those who have strayed.

Thank you Steven for being real.

I believe it will help others experience the same transformation you have!

2 Corinthians 5:17 (NKJV)

"Therefore, if anyone is in Christ, he is a new creation; old things have passed away; behold, all things have become new."

Pastor Qwest
Pastor Qwest Gatlin
Victory City Church

CHAPTER ONE

Steven's Journals

THE MISSION

"To bring revival to the church and demonstrate the Truth of God to the World" is a mission statement I wrote in one of my old prayer journals in my 20s.

This chapter is titled "Steven's Journals" as it comprises a collection of various entries I have written in my prayer journals over the course of 30 years. These entries include sermons, reflections, prayers, and prophecies. They also contain practical insights that I have gained through my many encounters with God and God's guidance as an overcomer in Christ in relation to sexual sin. For me that was homosexuality. For you, it may be something else. The biblical principles and spiritual practices that I present in this book serve as essential tools for achieving victory over any sin.

It's important to understand that sin is sin - regardless of how one may try to rationalize or justify it. If the Bible calls it a sin, it is a sin. Even if it's disguised as a cultural or civil rights issue, it still falls under the category of sin. No amount of embellishment with bright colors and glitter will change that, and there is no gold at the end of that rainbow. You can bawl, squall, beg and plead with God all day for change. But Jesus has already done everything necessary to address sin through His sacrifice on the cross, and there is no further action required on God's part.

The only answer for sin is repentance and faith in the blood of Jesus. Legally, our redemption in Christ is finished. It is up to us to 'appropriate' the things He bought and paid for on the cross in our life. 'Appropriate' means to make it your own, and take it as it is yours. The lifestyle of an overcomer is a daily walk of building a strong spirit, renewing the mind, and subduing the body through the Word and the Spirit of God.

There are several verses of scripture that I feel are Hallmark scriptures or golden texts in my life.

Acts 26:18-19; 13:36; 17:6 AMP, "To open their (spiritual) eyes so that they may turn from darkness to light. And from the power of Satan to GOD. That they may receive forgiveness and release from their sins and an inheritance among those who have been sanctified (set apart, made holy) by faith in me. So, King Agrippa, I (Steven Sluder) was not disobedient to the heavenly vision." I know this is the apostle Paul speaking here. But I like to insert my name in there. By no means am I even remotely close to anything the apostle was here on the earth. But every one of us has a heavenly call to respond to, and when we insert our name, we are accepting that call.

The thought had crossed my mind that one day I might author a book about my vision and call of God on my life. He has dealt with me and proven Himself to me in such a way that I have something to say about the life-changing power of His Word. And testify to the truth of God in me to this generation. I am to be like David who, in Acts 13:36 AMP, "served God's will and purpose to his own generation....." And Paul and Silas who "turned their world upside down...." Acts 17:6 AMP

THE VISION

When I was twelve years old, my family and I were at a service where Rev. Larry Moss was speaking. I responded to an altar call for those who felt called to the ministry. When hands were laid upon me,

I was slain in the spirit, the power of God went into me, and I lay on the floor and saw a vision of my life.

The vision had two parts. In the first part, I was standing in a wide-open space like a field and saw three very dark, evil spirits coming towards me. They were 1. Rejection/ Inferiority. 2. Drug/Alcohol addiction. 3. Sexual Perversion. They were coming towards me as John 10:10 KJV says, "To kill, steal, and destroy." As they came closer, a wall of transparent, cement-like blocks came up between us. Each block represented an area of my life. The evil spirits came up to the wall, but could not get through to me. They began looking for weak spots in the wall of my life. And eventually, they found areas that were weak and started trying to get in. The moment there was the slightest little opening, water began to seep in. Eventually, the hole got bigger and bigger and bigger, until the water was gushing in and surrounding me. The water level rose to the top of my chin, and I had the sense and fear of drowning. Just as the water reached the top of my mouth, suddenly, numerous hands appeared from behind me and started to gather the fragments of the broken wall, reassembling it piece by piece. As the wall was reconstructed, the water receded, ultimately disappearing altogether, and the various aspects of my life were strengthened once again.

In the second part of the vision, I was standing in another wide-open space. Only, this time I stood in front of a sea of people as far as the eye could see. There were people there from every race all over the earth.

That time of my life was exciting as I walked with God and heard from Him as a child. There was one more occasion around the same time in my life when God Spoke to me through a Pastor in Prophecy.

THE PROPHECY

"Those disappointments that have tried to hold you back in days gone by. And words and thoughts of others have been sent by your way that have tried to hold you back from flowing in that way. Those days are behind you, and they are gone forever more. Now, you just shout the victory. And know that the Lord is on your side. And you lift that voice in one accord and in praise to Him. And you will see your enemies flee. Yes, they will even go away from them. And so, you praise me with your voice, and you yield it as a vessel, and I will bless it. And the anointing will increase even double fold upon you as you walk faithfully."

Pastor Samson Doolin- Liberty World Outreach, Tulsa, Oklahoma.

The Word of My Testimony

During one of our counseling sessions in April 2001, Pastor Marty Blackwelder suggested that I write a book, and I owe much of my inspiration to him. So, here's my story. It all began when my parents, Janet Mae Smith and Paul Sluder, met in Bartlesville, Oklahoma, where Paul, a teenage evangelist, was conducting a revival in a church. At the time, they were 18 and 19 years old, and they got married soon after. A year later, on September 29, 1972, I was born, becoming the oldest of their three children. My younger siblings are my sister ReJeanna Jolliff and our brother Ben Sluder.

Our parents had gotten a hold of the Word of God by listening to Kenneth E. Hagin and graduated from Rhema Bible Training Center in 1978. Mom would teach us scripture through songs about healing and the fruit of the spirit by David Ingles. Eventually, we memorized entire chapters like Romans 8 and Psalm 91. We could quote them by memory. I was Born Again, baptized in the Holy Ghost, and spoke in tongues at the age of nine under the children's Ministries of Willie George (Gospel Bill), Ken Blount (Nicodemus), and Len Mink (Gospel Duck) at Kenneth Hagin's Camp meeting in 1981. We went to Kenneth Hagin Ministries Campmeeting every year. I grew up listening to ministers like Norvel Hayes, Fred Price, Charles Capps, and John Osteen.

As a teenager, my influences were Blaine Bartel, John George, and Ron Luce. We grew up under the anointing and learned the Word. God dealt with me as I grew. I received the call to ministry through the vision and prophecy in 1984 when I was 12. So I came into my teenage years on fire for God. I devoted my time to prayer, the Word, and church activities. We moved to Pennsylvania in the early 80s for my parents to take a ministry position in a church, where I went to the Conestoga Valley school district.

During Jr. and Sr. High school, I was the president of a Bible study club and led early morning prayer groups before class, which had never happened before in my school. And I even hosted prayer groups in my home.

During my high school years, God moved powerfully among us. Our meetings saw students being saved, healed, and filled with the Holy Spirit. As we continued to grow in our faith, the Lord led us to hold several all-night prayer gatherings in my home. Donna Ryan, a prayer Pastor from our Church in Lancaster, PA - The Worship Center, would guide and instruct us in prayer and intercession. Along with her husband Barry Ryan, they became spiritual parents to me.

I distinctly remember one all-night prayer meeting where the presence of God was so strong in my living room that some students were slain under the power of the Holy Spirit, while others knelt on the floor weeping and interceding fervently. All of this was happening while my family slept upstairs, unaware of the divine encounter taking place. It was a powerful demonstration of God's sovereignty, and we were all completely surrendered to His will, hungry for more of Him - just like how Jesus yielded himself to the Father in Hebrews 5:7. We were not concerned about what others were thinking, but were instead totally yielded to the Holy Spirit.

We moved from Pennsylvania for Dad to start a new church in Chickasha, Oklahoma in 1989. I was in my junior year of High School. I started a new Bible club and prayer group, but there seemed to be some oppression in the school, and it had a tough time growing. Before long, I found out there was an English teacher who was a self-proclaimed witch. I was not in her class, but one day I was led to go witness to her after school. I approached her with the Gospel, told her Jesus loved her, died for her sins, and would free her from her witchcraft and His power was greater than the powers that she thought she had. She rejected what I shared. As I left, I prayed, "God, either save her or move her out of this school." At the start of my Senior year, she did not return. She quit and went to teach in another school district. In my senior year, the Bible club and Prayer group did much better than the year before.

I graduated from High school in 1991 and moved to Tulsa to attend Rhema Bible College. However, I did not finish my first year because I got involved in a homosexual relationship. At first, it was strictly sexual. Eventually, it became a committed relationship, so neither of us finished our first year.

Eventually, I returned to Rhema, finished two years, and finally graduated in 2001. After completing my studies, I landed a job as a Worship Leader at New Wine Christian Center, a church in Pennsylvania, where Pastors Barry and Donna Ryan were leading. Donna, who had been my prayer mentor during my teenage years, was part of the pastoral team. I worked there as a staff member for a year and a half, and it was during this time that I began writing this book from my office. However, when I realized what God was calling me to do, I told the Lord, "Forget this! Use somebody else."

Regrettably, another ungodly same-sex relationship derailed me. I left my position at the church and high-tailed it straight to New York City until January 2007. Just like Jonah, I ran from what God wanted me to do. NYC was my Tarshish. While I lived in Manhattan, I ran from God and the call of God in my life by living a full-out homosexual life. I lived a very promiscuous, polyamorous lifestyle. It was filled with drug and alcohol abuse. I can remember having drug overdoses and somehow winding up in the hospital. One time I walked home to my apartment in Harlem from a hospital in Washington Heights because I did not have money for a cab or my METROcard for the subway. I had lost my wallet the night before.

Once, while on the dance floor of a popular nightclub in Chelsea, I overdosed and was escorted out of the building through the back door. I found myself passed out and detoxing on the street, unaware of how long I had been there. When I finally regained consciousness, I made my way back to Harlem feeling hungover.

During my time in Manhattan, I worked at two salons. The first was an internship at Frederic Fekkai in the Chanel building in midtown. The second was a trendy boutique European salon located on W. 16th Street in Chelsea. My boss would let me leave the salon sometimes to go work on photo shoots for the day. Despite being able to go on the floor and receive ongoing education, I often showed up high on drugs after being out all night. Consequently, my boss canceled my appointments and assigned me to do laundry instead of working with clients.

One time he sat me down on the lounge chair in the lobby that faced the street. A homeless lady was walking by, and he told me if I didn't quit, that I was going to wind up on the streets like her. She was the Chelsea neighborhood homeless, prostitute, and junkie. I would do good for a little while. Then the next party would come along, and I would go out again and wind up in another tailspin of being up and out for days. Thankfully, my boss at the time cared enough for me to want to help. He could have easily fired me from my job. I also had a third job working for a couple of famous nightlife impresarios who kept me burning the candle at both ends. They had me running between Manhattan and Fire Island in the summertime almost every weekend. Despite my addiction, NYC was an amazing experience career-wise. I had the privilege of working with famous hairstylists and assisting with high-profile photoshoots for magazines and commercials. But the three evil spirits I saw in my vision had gained full entry into my life just like God showed me. Except, I was not thinking at all about my vision or the things of God. The only thing on my mind was partying, drinking, drugging, and sleeping around. I went from one fix to another. One addiction to the other. One hook-up to another. Life was empty, but I always wanted more. I could not get enough. Sin was fun for a season.

In August 2006, I received a serious medical diagnosis, and the first people I informed were my parents. I immediately called them in Tyler, Texas, and shared everything with them. I am grateful I knew who to turn to. After a long conversation with my father, he asked me if I was ready to come back home, to which I replied with a resounding "no!" I believed that I could handle the situation alone, but in reality, I couldn't. Over the next four months, I attempted to quit my addiction on my own, but it had too strong of a hold on me. I was too far gone to stop, and I required intervention; otherwise, I would have ended up homeless or worse, dead.

In December of that same year, shortly before Christmas, I finally reached out to my dad and confessed that I needed help and was ready to come back home. At the time, my dad was driving an old Ford F150 truck and quickly made arrangements to pick up my brother Ben in Ohio before hitting the road to NYC. I was in denial they were genuinely coming, and I went on a bender the night before they arrived. But sure enough, they arrived in front of my building in Washington Heights where parking was usually a nightmare for normal size vehicles, much less a truck and trailer! However, miraculously, there was enough space for the truck and trailer to park right in front of my building on 187th and Broadway. It seemed impossible to find that much space, but to this day, I am convinced that one of my Ministering Spirits held that parking spot open for them until they arrived. We will talk more about angels later.

So, the three of us loaded the truck and trailer with my belongings and slowly made our way home. We dropped Ben off and decided to spend Christmas of 2006 with him and his family. Then my father and I left to go back to Tyler, Texas. . Unfortunately, moving to Texas did not change my old ways. From 2007 until 2015 I continued to live like I did when I was in New York. I even moved to Dallas at one point for a year and a half. My lifestyle in Dallas was the same as it was in NYC. In June 2014, I checked in and did 30 days in rehab. In

2015 I was diagnosed with testicular cancer and spent 2015 to 2016 in chemotherapy. Now, I want to make it clear that I do not believe God puts sickness and disease on you to teach you a lesson. He will never put anything back on you that He has redeemed you from through the blood of Jesus. It did, however, give me plenty of time to think. Cancer brought me face to face with life and death. I thought about what would happen to me if it took my life.

During that time in chemo, I recommitted my life to Jesus. I told God "If you will heal me and bring me out of this, I will spend the rest of my life fulfilling your plan and purpose." And He did! It was at that moment, when I gave my life back to God, that I entered the second phase of the vision that I had when I was 12. The first phase of what God showed me was behind me! The last 20-plus years of my adult life have been of God dealing with me, and me running from God. Then God dealt with me, and me running again. I knew I was supposed to author this book at New Wine Christian Center. But I put it off. At times I would yield to God, and other times I would yield to the flesh. Over that period, I have been in and out of ungodly relationships, moved around the country, running from my family and the call of God on my life. Yet, God was patient with me and dealt with me repeatedly and again! Thank God for His grace and His mercy. He brought me through it. I can look back now and see his hand on my life even then.

The language of the Spirit

I will never forget one specific time God dealt with me in my mid-twenties in the 90s. I experienced a powerful encounter with God that remains vivid in my memory. At the time, my father was serving as pastor of a church in Chickasha, Oklahoma which later relocated to Tuttle. During a guest speaker's sermon on the Glory of God, an altar call was made, and I responded. As the speaker laid his hands on me, I was overwhelmed by the power of God and found myself suspended in a trance-like state. I saw a bright flash of light and was completely immobilized, unable to move my body. An example of this would be in Acts 10:10 KJV when "Peter went on the rooftop to pray and fell into a trance."

A vision can come in several forms.

1. An inward vision you see in the spirit with the eyes of your spirit (Acts 10:1-3) KJV

2. A trance is when your physical senses are suspended. (Acts 10:10) KJV

3. A vision where your physical eyes are open to see into the spirit realm. (Acts 9:8) KJV

I was in a trance having an inward vision while I stood there for almost three hours. The fire of God came and sat on top of my head and settled all the way down in my stomach and burned inside of me. God was burning away all the chaff and putting in me the fire of God to do His will. I also saw the second part of the vision that I had when I was twelve. I was standing in front of a sea of people, and this time I was laying hands on them, and the fire of God was coming out of my hands into them. My mother and another lady in the church stayed with me after everyone else was gone. They said I was sweating while I stood there frozen with my eyes closed. I wept under the power of God for three hours.

My mother remembered when the Lord told Brother Hagin to lay hands on someone who had fallen into a trance, and they would come out of it. I remember her saying "in the name of Jesus" as she touched me and the power came out of me. They put a chair behind me since no one was there to catch me and I fell back limp on the chair. Somehow, they were able to get me to the car. Still weeping and unable to speak. Like Ezekiel, I was struck dumb. It was like my tongue was stuck to the roof of my mouth. (Ezekiel 3:26.)

Not until the following day did I come out of my dumb state. I had been in the tangible presence of God. That was such a powerful experience that lasted such a long time at that moment. I thank God for those incredible experiences, He showed Himself strong on my behalf. As a young person, such experiences left a deep impression on me. However, it's important to note that visions, dreams, prophecy, and the Word of God manifesting in one's life are all contingent upon certain conditions that must be met. Although your spirit changes instantly when you get saved, transforming your soul and body requires a conscious effort on your part. It's by applying the truths embedded in your recreated human spirit to your daily life that you can truly benefit from these experiences in God.

God doesn't just instantaneously change you; there is a divine aspect as well as a human aspect to everything. We must learn to work in harmony with God on a daily basis. That is the primary message of this book. I am grateful for the amazing experiences that God grants us through visions and dreams.

Those are the languages of the Holy Ghost. But what happens on Monday morning when I am not feeling fire or seeing light from heaven? Victory is a practical, everyday walk. And let us be honest, visions and dreams do not happen daily. The Christian walk is a walk of Faith. It is a step-by-step process of change that takes time, discipline, and a lifetime of the Word of God and Prayer. This book is based on my experience. But you cannot take my word for it. You must decide for yourself if you want to be free from any sexual sin that binds you. Get out a Bible, a pen, and a journal, and let God speak to you.

Notes

Notes

_____

_____

_____

_____

_____

_____

_____

_____

_____

_____

_____

_____

_____

_____

_____

_____

_____

Notes

Notes

Chapter Two

IDENTIFICATION

WHO IS THE REAL 'I'?

In this chapter, I want to deal with the subjects of Spirit, soul, and body. As well as identification with Christ.

1 Thessalonians 5:23 KJV, "I pray God your whole spirit (pneuma), soul (psyche) and body (soma) be preserved blameless until the coming of our Lord Jesus Christ." The Bible breaks humanity down into three dimensions. Spirit, soul, and body. We are a triune being. All three are distinct in function and nature. Yet, work together to make one person.

1 Corinthians 9:27 KJV, "But, I keep my body under, and bring it into subjection..."

Here we see a definite separation of Paul's body from the real him and the influence of the real person upon the body.

2 Peter 1:13 KJV, "I think it meet (right) as long as I am in this tabernacle (tent, body) to stir you up by way of remembrance..." Peter made a clear observation that his body was only a tabernacle. Not the real him. And the real him lived inside the body. We see a greater sense of identification with something other than what we see or who we are on the outside.

1 Thessalonians 4:4 KJV, "That each one of you should know how to possess (manage, control) his own body in sanctification and honor."

We can see that the body is not the actual "I." Who were Peter and Paul referring to? It is the spirit that lives within the body. "The hidden man of the heart" 1 Peter 3:4. We are spirits, we have a soul, and we live in a body. The spirit man is our contact with the spirit world for the purpose of direct communication with God. Our body is our contact with the natural world for the purpose of direct communication with the natural realm. We are not bodies having a spiritual experience. We are spirits having an earthly, natural experience.

We use the word "I" loosely. Not really thinking about whom we are talking about. We use the word from the standpoint of the body. "I am tired" or "I have a headache." Sometimes it is used soulishly. "I am depressed" or, "I think so." But words spoken from the standpoint of the born-again recreated human spirit will develop it to rule and dominate over the soul and body. Otherwise, words spoken from the standpoint of your soul or body will weaken the spirit and cause it to be led by reason or the senses. Obviously, if your body is tired, you will say that it is. We are not to deny the existence of physical conditions. We are, however, to deny physical conditions the RIGHT to exist through the power of the Word and the Holy Spirit. Here we are talking about subduing the body and its ungodly desires. There is a scriptural way to do that.

THE CONSEQUENCE OF YOUR WORDS

Who is the real "I" , the spirit man? And how do we develop a strong identity with it? 2 Corinthians 5:17 KJV, says "Therefore if any man be in Christ, he is a new creature. Old things are passed away; behold all things are become new." The real "I" is a New Creation.

ripture speaks of a new nature in your spirit. Galatians 6:15 'or neither is circumcision anything, nor uncircumcision. But a new creation (which is the result of a new birth-a spiritual transformation- a new nature in Christ Jesus)" [AMP]

If I have a new nature in Christ in my spirit, but my mind is still thinking one way, and my desires in my body are responding to it. How do I tap into the new nature within me? It starts with the words of your mouth and the part of you that you identify with. What part of you is dominating? Is it your spirit, your soul, or your body? Proverbs 18:20-21 KJV, "A man's stomach shall be satisfied with the fruit of his mouth. He will be satisfied with the consequence of his words. Death and life are in the power of the tongue. And those who love it and indulge it will eat its fruits and bear the consequence of their words."

We speak into existence who and what we are. We do it every day. Everything you say brings life or death. The first thing you must do to establish your identity is to correct your words. Speak according to 1 Corinthians 6:17-20 KJV, that "I am united to the Lord. I am one spirit with Him. Therefore, I flee fornication."

2 Peter 1:3-4 KJV, "According as His divine power hath given unto us all things that pertain unto life and godliness.... that ye might be partakers of the divine nature having escaped the corruption that is in this world through lust." Corruption and deception always come through lust. This is exactly how Satan and his demonic spirits work.

It is possible to transform how you have labeled yourself, and how the world has labeled you, into the image of God. 2 Peter declares it by partaking of God's divine nature within us. The nature of Christ is in me, and it is the hope of Glory and of better things to come. Colossians 1:27 KJV, "To whom God would make known what the riches of the glory of this mystery is among the gentiles, which is Christ in you the hope of glory."

I will speak more about the glory later. For now, I want to focus on the spirit man.

Identifying with the nature of God inside ourselves, and developing the spirit man in Christ is one key to walking in victory over homosexuality or any sexual sin. Begin right now, right where you are…even if you are in the middle of the situation, and it is still happening around you. Now is the time to speak from your born-again, recreated human spirit and say "NO!" Do not identify with anything other than who God's Word says you are.

Building the strength of your spirit man to rule over your soul and body through your words, is like building your physical muscles through lifting weights. If you want to build strong chest muscles, you isolate that part of your body. This principle in the natural is parallel to the spirit realm in making your Spirit strong in an area where you are weak. Isolate your words and build your strength in a particular area. Find scripture that pertains to your situation and confess it over your life, for instance. Joel 3:10 says "Let the weak say I am strong" We could say 1 Peter 2:24 KJV, like this "Let the sick say I am healed" whatever the situation is, confess the answer in the face of the problem. If you have a weakness in loving a person, according to Galatians 5:22 KJV, you could say that "The fruit of the spirit in me is love." Start speaking to yourself… here is an example "I have been created spirit, soul, and body to produce and bring forth life. My born-again human spirit rules and dominates over my soul and body. My sexual desires come in line with the Word of God."

AS A MAN THINKETH

Thoughts that we focus on, produce actions. Actions produce habits. Habits produce lifestyle. Lifestyle produces destiny. THERE IS DESTINY IN YOUR THOUGHTS.

A renewed mind is a conductor of the born-again, recreated human spirit's power.

There's an old saying, "You are what you eat." Thoughts are to your soul, what food is to your body. In other words, you are what you think. Proverbs 23:7 KJV, "For as he thinketh in his heart so is he..." The word thinketh in Hebrew is <u>SHAAR</u>. It means to act as the keeper of a door or gate to a city.

The gateway to your soul is your thoughts, and the thoughts you entertain directly impact your spirit and physical being. As gatekeepers, we have the responsibility to control what enters the gates of our minds, just as a city gatekeeper would control who enters the city.

Proverbs 25:28 KJV, says, "He who has no rule over his own spirit is like a city that is broken down and without walls." Merely having a thought does not mean it is one you conjured up...from inside yourself. Thoughts are not facts, that is why you must make sure to train your thought life according to the Word of God. If you entertain thoughts of sexual impurity, you open your entire being to spirits of perversion. The crucial part of the word entertain is "enter." What you use as "enter"-tainment is allowing something entrance into you. This is how devils and demonic spirits operate. When you dwell on thoughts, good or evil, this allows them entrance. This is how people are demonized. They entertain thoughts that are contrary to the Word.

Evil Spirits are not so much concerned about the air as we make them out to be. They are more concerned about weak minds when they are not renewed by the Word of GOD to prey upon. Ephesians 2:2-3 KJV, "Wherein time past ye walked according to the course of this world. According to the prince of the power of the air that now worketh in the children of disobedience. Among whom we all had our conversation in times past in the lust of our flesh <u>and of the mind</u> ..." 2 Corinthians 4:4 KJV, also says "...in whom the god of this world hath <u>blinded the minds</u> of them which believe not. "

The *way* a man thinks is the entry door to darkness or light. The *only* thing that can enlighten the spirit and soul of man is the Word of God. Psalms 119:130 KJV, "The entrance of thy words giveth light."

Paul said in Romans 12:2 KJV, to be "...Transformed by the renewing of your <u>MINDS</u>."

Speak this out loud to yourself right now... "I am a spirit, I walk in the spirit, and I do not fulfill the lusts of the flesh. I live and move in the ways of the Spirit, not in the ways of the flesh. I am filled with the fruit of the spirit of self-control, and I control my thoughts. Any thoughts that are contrary to the Word of God do not control me. Destiny is in my thoughts. The fruit of the spirit is the divine nature of GOD. And I am a partaker of His divine nature."

Your words allow or forbid access into your spirit, soul, and body. A spirit that is fed God's Word by meditating on it will become stronger than your soul and body.

When your thinking changes, it will affect your whole being. 3 John 2 KJV, "Beloved I wish above all things that thou mayest prosper and be in health even as thy soul prospers." Aligning my thoughts and speech with God's Word leads to enlightenment and aligns my desires with His will. Another fascinating concept I have discovered about thoughts is the meaning of "thinketh" in Proverbs 23:7 KJV, which refers to the responsibility of acting as a gatekeeper. The thoughts I entertain serve as the doorposts of my mind, allowing either godly or worldly influences to enter. The Lord has taught me a valuable lesson about the doorposts of the mind.

Let us read Exodus 12:3,5,7,13, and 23 KJV

Vs. 3: "Tell all the congregation of Israel, on the tenth day of this month they shall take every man a lamb for each house...

Vs. 5: "Your lamb shall be without blemish..."

Vs. 7 "They shall take of the blood and put it on the two side posts on the lintel (above the door space) of the houses in which they shall eat (the Passover Lamb)."

Vs. 13 "The blood shall be a token or a sign to you upon the doorposts of the houses where you are. That when I see the blood, I will pass over you. And no plague shall be upon you to destroy you when I smite the land of Egypt."

Vs, 23 "For the Lord will pass through to slay the Egyptians and when he sees the blood upon the lintel and the two side posts, the Lord will pass over the door and will not allow the destroyer to come into your houses to slay you.

The Old Covenant provides us with a blueprint, a foreshadowing of what was to come in the New Covenant - a superior covenant. . I do not subscribe to replacement theology, which suggests that the Church has replaced Israel. Instead, the Church embodies the spiritual congregation of Israel, having been grafted into the promise and blessing of Abraham. As heirs of the covenant, we are entitled to its inheritance, and Jesus is the unblemished and faultless Lamb.

1 Peter 1:19 KJV, "But, with the precious blood of Christ, as of a lamb without blemish and without spot."

We are to apply the blood of the lamb of GOD to the doorposts of our house, the mind, by faith. Hebrews 9:11-14 KJV, "But, Christ being come a High Priest of good things to come by a greater and more perfect tabernacle not made with hands not of this building; Neither by the blood of goats and calves, but by his own blood he entered in once into the Holy Place having obtained eternal redemption for us. For if the blood of bulls and goats, and the ashes of a heifer sprinkling the unclean, sanctifieth to the purifying of the flesh: HOW MUCH MORE SHALL THE BLOOD OF CHRIST, who through the eternal spirit offered himself without spot to GOD, PURGE YOUR CONSCIENCE FROM DEAD WORKS TO SERVE THE LIVING GOD."

By faith, we apply the blood of Jesus to the doorposts of our minds and our consciences. Hebrews 10:22 KJV, says we are to "Draw near with a true heart, in full assurance of faith having our hearts sprinkled from an evil conscience..." Oh, the Blood of Jesus. It will never lose its power! It is the only answer to sexual perversion.

Renewing the mind

Romans 12:1-2 NKJV

"I beseech you therefore, brethren, by the mercies of God, that you present your bodies a living sacrifice, holy, acceptable to God, which is your reasonable service. And do not be conformed to this world, but be transformed by the renewing of your mind, that you may prove what is that good and acceptable and perfect will of God."

PROVERBS 25:28

KJ21

"He that hath no rule over his own spirit is like a city that is broken down and without walls."

The term "renew" is not commonly associated with the mind, but rather with renewing a subscription, such as for a magazine, Hulu, or Netflix. When a subscription to an online streaming service is renewed, the previous subscription has expired and needs updating. Similarly, our minds can also become outdated due to our sinful nature, and in order to renew it, we must engage in meditating on and speaking the Word of God. By doing so, our minds can become new again, just as they were when they were created.

Ephesians 4:23-24, KJV

Tree of Life Version

23 "be renewed in the spirit of your mind, 24 and put on the new self—created to be like God in true righteousness and holiness."

How does transformation happen? Because I diligently *speak the Word* over myself and say "In the Name of Jesus, I plead the Blood of Jesus over my mind. I forget the past and leave it behind." I bring every thought captive to the obedience of Christ by remembering who I am in Him. And by faith, with my words, I apply the blood to the doorposts of my mind.

I reject any influence from the destroyer within me. According to John 10:10, the devil sends destructive thoughts to kill, steal, and destroy. However, I have applied the blood of Jesus to my mind, and as a result, the destroyer cannot gain access to me. I take responsibility as the gatekeeper of my mind by rejecting negative thoughts and replacing them with God's Word, which illuminates my mind.

Psalms119:130 KJV, says "The entrance of thy words giveth light."

Entertaining thoughts of sexual sin that contradict the Word of God lead to darkness. Instead, focusing on the Word of God illuminates our thoughts with His truth. By applying the blood of Jesus to our minds, we keep the destroyer at bay. It is essential to practice this every time a thought arises. This is precisely what James 4:7 means: to submit to God, resist the devil, and he will flee from you. The word "flee" denotes running away in terror.

Many Christians struggle to make the devil flee because they fail to live a life fully submitted to God. They do not renew their minds or meditate on His Word, which makes it difficult to resist the devil's schemes. Rather than prioritizing their personal spiritual growth, they yearn to be used by God as intercessors for national or global matters. However, they have not yet learned the importance of having a disciplined thought life or denying their flesh in private. As a result, God cannot trust them with sensitive information because they are too preoccupied with satisfying their fleshly desires.

God's definition of meditation is different from the world's. Their definition is to clear your mind and relax through transcendental meditation or yoga, which is nothing more than a form of Hindu meditation. No Christian has any business doing that. You cannot have yoga without Hinduism. And you cannot have Hinduism without yoga. Historically, yoga and its poses are religious positions of worship to false gods, and false idols and it cannot be done in a way that is not spiritual. That is why it is coming in the name of Christianity and infiltrating churches. Yoga is a form of worship to false pagan Hindu gods and is done to increase your "self" awareness. Yahweh's definition of meditation is to fill your mind with his Word by speaking it aloud repeatedly to yourself. Aligning your doshas and chakras to become more self-aware is deception and is the arm of the flesh. Attempting to resolve a spiritual problem with physical methods leads to the body taking control. Only the Word of God and the Holy Spirit can properly align our spirit, soul, and body, resulting in genuine peace of mind and emotional stability. True emotional healing can only come through meditating on scripture. Ironically, the world is attempting to raise awareness of something the Bible instructs us to crucify.

Joshua 1:8

King James Version

8 "This book of the law shall not depart out of thy mouth; but thou shalt meditate therein day and night, that thou mayest observe to do according to all that is written therein: for then thou shalt make thy way prosperous, and then thou shalt have good success." The picture that this passage of scripture paints for us here is like a cow chewing his cud. A cow has several stomachs that regurgitate its food for them to chew again. We are to continually chew on the Word. If you clear your mind and relax the way the world teaches you to do it, the enemy will find plenty of things to fill it with. But if you fill your mind with the Word it leaves no room for any of his deceptions. Psalm 1:2 KJV "But his delight is in the law of the Lord. And in His law doth he meditate day and night." The world meditates their way for a false sense of temporary peace.

We are told to "Let the peace of God rule in your hearts" by letting "the Word of Christ dwell in you richly..." Colossians 3:15, 16.

Psalm 119:15 NIV "I meditate on your precepts and consider your ways."

Isaiah 59:21 New King James Version

21 "As for Me," says the Lord, "this is My covenant with them: My Spirit who is upon you, and My words which I have put in your

mouth, shall not depart from your mouth, nor from the mouth of your descendants, says the Lord, "from this time and forevermore."

The devil is the destroyer. But He is a defeated foe. Homosexuality is a sin. And the wages of sin is death. But you can avoid it by applying the blood by faith against him, and he will flee from you in terror. He hates to see the blood of Jesus on you. It reminds him of his defeat at Calvary.

Revelations 12:11 KJV, says "They overcame him by the Blood of the Lamb, by the word of their testimony, and they loved not their life even unto death."

We are overcomers through the Blood of Jesus. The #1 Key to living an overcoming lifestyle is the Blood of Jesus!

SUBDUING THE BODY

Now I will focus on the tabernacle, which represents the tent of the authentic "I," including the human spirit and God, the Holy Spirit. 1 Corinthians 6:17-20 KJV, "For he that is joined to the Lord is one spirit. Flee Fornication. Every sin that a man doeth is without the body; but he that committeth fornication sinneth against his own body. What? Know ye not that your body is the temple of the Holy Ghost, which is in you, which ye have of GOD. And ye are not your own? For ye are bought with a price. Therefore, GLORIFY GOD IN YOUR BODY AND IN YOUR SPIRIT which are God's"

1 Thessalonians 4:3-4 KJV, "For this is the will of GOD, even your sanctification, that ye should abstain from fornication. that every one of you should know how to possess his vessel (body) in sanctification and honor.

The Greek word for body is SOMA which means slave. You must first master your own body before you master the body of Christ. The body is to come under submission to the spirit man through a mind that is renewed with the Word of God. Paul said in 1 Corinthians

9:27 "But, (like a boxer) I strictly discipline my body and make it my slave..." [AMP]

A helpful analogy to understand this concept is that the spirit is like the driver, the soul is like the engine, and the body is like the vehicle. People who identify solely based on their physical body focus on the flesh. They become focused on their soul if they have not renewed their mind. However, those who cultivate their inner being by thinking and speaking God's Word become focused on their spirit. The soul and the body were never intended to govern a person's life. When they do, it leads to a collision.

Therefore, my sexual urges and longings are subject under my control. While I may experience natural attractions and physical arousal due to past experiences or sensory stimuli, I am able to manage them. The manifestation of self-control is a fruit of the Spirit within me, and enables me to do so.

Paul said in 2 Corinthians 4:13 KJV, to release the spirit of faith within you by believing and speaking exactly like God does. "...We also believe therefore we also speak." In Romans 4:17 KJV, God "....Calleth those things which be not as though they were."

So, I say that "I am a spirit, I have a soul, I live in a body. I am born of GOD. And I am an overcomer of the world. I have crucified the old nature, and it died with Christ. I have a new nature. The nature of GOD is in me. I am His workmanship. Created in Christ unto good works that GOD hath before ordained that I should walk in them. I will walk in all that GOD has before ordained for me to walk in. I am seated with Christ in Heavenly places at the right hand of GOD, above every name that can be named. The name of homosexuality is under my feet. I am in Him, and He is in me. I am filled with the Godhead. He is the head of all principalities and powers. Therefore, I am above them too. If I have been raised with Christ, I seek and set my mind on those things that are above. As far as the world is concerned, I have died. I am clothed with the new spiritual self. This is GOD's will for me that I am consecrated. I possess and control my own body. I put on the new nature created in true righteousness and holiness. I walk in the spirit and do not fulfill the lusts of the flesh. I am being transformed by the renewing of my mind. And I am proving what is the good, acceptable, and perfect, will of GOD!"

Make these thoughts your thoughts. And these words your words.

We need to remind ourselves every day. I heard Kenneth E Hagin say one time that 'renewing the mind' was like combing or styling your hair. You must do it every day. Sometimes two or three times a day. Just like hair maintenance, keeping your mind renewed is constant upkeep. You must do it repeatedly. When the morning comes, wake up and do it again. Sometimes we check our hair in the mirror many times daily and only renew our minds once a week!

Transformation *is* possible. It starts inside of you by changing your thought life and lining your words up with God's Word. Then Hebrews 4:12 happens. "For the Word of GOD is quick, and powerful, and sharper than any two-edged sword. Piercing even to the dividing asunder of soul and spirit, and of the joints and marrow, and is a discerner of the thoughts and intents of the heart." Meditating the Word will put your three-fold being in proper alignment and will help you to discern between right and wrong thoughts and intentions.

Ruling and reigning

Romans 5:17 says "For if by one man's offense death reigned by one; much more they who receive abundance of grace and of the gift of righteousness shall reign in life by one, Jesus Christ." That is me! I have received an abundance of grace.

2 Corinthians 5:21 says I have been made in right standing with God.

In Christ we are to rule and reign in this life. I rule over my spirit. I rule over my soul. I have a sound mind, a disciplined thought life, a strong will, and stable emotions. I rule over my body. My feelings and desires come in line with the Word of God. My body does not rule me. It does not dictate to me who or what I am. My sexual desires do not rule me. They come in line with the Word when I confess it daily.

Ecclesiastes 8:4 "Where the Word of a king is there is power." I am a king in Him. When I speak in line with His will, it carries power. Just like Samuel. God "did not let none of his words fall to the ground." 1 Samuel 3:19. When His words become my words then "I shall decree a thing and it shall be established." Job 22:28. Revelation 1:5-6 says that I am washed in the blood of Jesus and made a king and a priest unto God. Daily rule and reign over your soul and body through God's Word.

The second key to living an overcoming lifestyle is our words. Revelations 12:1 "They overcame him by the Blood of the Lamb and the word of their testimony."

My testimony is that I have been delivered from sin!

My testimony is who Jesus has made me in HIM!

Union with Christ:

The main focus of our conversation revolves around identity. Identifying with Christ involves becoming indistinguishable, and being regarded as one and the same. From the moment Jesus was crucified until He was seated at the Father's right hand, He acted as our representative. We are identified with His death, burial, resurrection, and ascension.

2 Corinthians 5:17 KJV says "Therefore if any man be in Christ, he is a new creature; old things are passed away; behold, all things are new." I like the way the NEB translation puts it. "When anyone is united with Christ, there is a new world; the old order has gone, and a new order has already begun."

A new creature means a new species of being that never existed before.

John 15:5 William's translation says "...whoever remains in union with me and I in union with him will bear abundant fruit...." When we are born again and the Holy Spirit takes up residence in us, we are vitally united with Jesus, and our identity changes. I like to call this cross-heredity. My heredity and identity now go back to the cross. Of course, I still have silver hair and blue eyes like my earthly father. But, as far as the sinful nature is concerned, I am now a partaker of divine nature.

2 Peter 1:4. And my new bloodline begins and ends with Jesus. That includes generational or family curses. Once I am born again, I have a new bloodline and those curses no longer apply to me. Galatians 3:13 says that Jesus redeemed me from EVERY curse. The only thing left after that is to renew my mind to the Word of God.

1 Corinthians 6:17 KJV says "But he that is joined to the Lord is one spirit" The Living Bible says, "But if you give yourself to the Lord, you and Christ are joined together as one person." Ephesians 2:15 says that Jesus abolished the enmity between us and God "... for to make in himself of twain one new man..." In Christ, we are a new person, and the old man/woman is gone. Romans 6:6 says that "our old man is crucified with Him!" When Jesus died, I died. Death means separation. Spiritual death is eternal separation from God. Physical death is the separation of the spirit from the body. This death of the old man means the separation of us from our sinful nature! It was nailed to the cross with Jesus when we made him our Lord. And if we died with Him, then Romans 6:4-5 says we were also buried and risen with him in new life. "For if we have been planted together in the likeness of His death, we shall be also in the likeness of his resurrection." Thank God when He died, I died.

Galatians 2:20 KJV, says "I am crucified with Christ: nevertheless, I live; yet not I, but Christ liveth in me." When He was made alive, I was made alive. And, when He arose, I arose! But do not stop there. Ephesians 2:1 and 5 says that when He was quickened, I was quickened. Verse 6 says "And hath raised us up together and made us sit together in heavenly places in Christ Jesus." God went even a step further and gave us the same seat of authority he gave Jesus. Ephesians 1:21-22 says we are seated with Him "far above all principality, and power, and might, and dominion, and every name that is named not only in this world but also in that which is to come. And hath put all things under His feet..."

Well, if we are the body of Christ, His hands, and His feet. That means they are under my feet too. The name of addiction is under my feet. The name of sexual perversion is under my feet. The name of sin and all the effects of sin are under my feet! Just because a particular problem or issue was passed down from generation to generation does not mean it has to be true for me. We are talking about the curse of sin. Not physical attributes.

Our redemption is three-fold. We are redeemed from spiritual death (eternal separation from God), sickness and disease, poverty, and lack. That means the buck stops here. My identity is in Christ! The old Steven is dead, and I am seated with Jesus in heavenly places far above Satan, his lies, and all his cohorts. Homosexuality is under my feet! This is another great key to living the lifestyle of an overcomer. Knowing who we are in Christ. Knowing I am not who the world, Satan, or my flesh says I am.

When you build a strong identity with who you are *in Him*, your spiritual stamina to stand against the wiles of the devil is stronger. You are not as susceptible to giving in to temptation. Temptation is still very real. The enemy will try to throw everything he has at you. Isaiah 54:17 New King James Version says, 17 "No weapon formed against you shall prosper, and every tongue which rises against you in judgment You shall condemn. This is the heritage of the servants of the Lord, and their righteousness is from Me, Says the Lord." Hallelujah, my own righteousness is as filthy rags. But now my righteousness is of Him. Sexual perversion is a weapon formed against us to abort the plan of God for our life!

Philemon 1:6 BRG "That the communication of thy faith may become effectual by the acknowledging of every good thing which is in you in Christ Jesus." Say what God says about you! Not what the enemy is saying. Acknowledge your identity in Christ by confessing 'who I am in Him' realities every day.

Notes

Notes

Notes

Notes

Chapter Three

THE TRUTH OF GOD

What is Reality?

What we are looking at in this book is how heavenly truth changes earthly realities. 2 Corinthians 4:18 KJV, says "While we look not at the things which are seen, but at the things which are not seen. For the things which are seen are temporal; but the things which are not seen are eternal." The verse discusses two dimensions of existence - the visible and the invisible. Although we inhabit the tangible world, there are intangible aspects that elude our senses. However, this is the reality of our earthly existence. How can we learn to perceive and access the unseen elements and manifest them in our lives?

Jesus said in John 17:17 KJV, "Sanctify them through thy truth. Thy word is truth." Jesus teaches that God's Word is the ultimate authority for discerning the truth of any matter. Recently, the phrase "living MY truth" or "their truth" has become popular. However, the truth is not subjective, and it is not something that can be personalized. Instead, there is only one Truth, and any other perspective is just an opinion. We should always refer to God's Word to resolve any uncertainties we have and to live our lives based on its Truth. Therefore, regardless of the circumstances on earth, we can seek a higher reality by turning to God's Word. When we embrace and act on this higher reality, it surpasses and transforms the earthly reality.

A good friend of mine Pastor Leigh Ann Soesbee said one time that "kingdom mentality is my reality." We can change earthly, natural reality in our lives with the Word of God. Dad Hagin used to say "when the natural comes in contact with the supernatural something must give. And it will not be the supernatural."

So, what does God's Word say about homosexuality? 1 Thessalonians 4:3 KJV, "For this is the will of GOD, even your sanctification, that ye should abstain from fornication." There is a law called the law of first mention. It says when something is first said that thing is set in motion. And it sets a precedent, and any deviation from its original course is to digress from its original state. Genesis 1:27 KJV, "So GOD created man in His own image. In the Image of GOD created he him. Male and female created he them."

Matthew 19:4 KJV, "And he answered and said unto them, have ye not read, that he which made them at the beginning made them male and female..."

Paul summarizes the issue to the church by saying in 1 Corinthians 6:9-10 KJV, "... Be not deceived, neither fornicators..., shall inherit the kingdom of GOD."

There is a lot more we could say here. I am keeping it simple and letting the Word speak for itself. In these four scriptures you can see what God's will is as it is expressed through Jesus, then Paul to the church, and the law of first mention in Genesis.

What is reality then? According to the teachings of God's Word, truth is the foundation. When we acknowledge and embrace this truth, reflect on it, and apply it to our lives, our perceptions and experiences of reality will shift. Our thoughts, emotions, and aspirations must align with the Word, and a Kingdom mindset will become our new reality, one that transcends the fleeting nature of the physical world. Through the power of the Word, our souls can be saved.

James 1:21 AMP, "So get rid of all uncleanness and all that remains of wickedness. And with a humble spirit receive the word (of GOD) which implanted (actually rooted in your heart), can save your souls."

Meditating on the Word is the only way to get it rooted and grounded inside of you. God is not going to do it for you. You must sit down, open your Bible, and put it in your mouth! Recently, I overheard someone making a questionable prophecy that included a non-scriptural statement. They told the recipient that God would renew their mind, but I must be blunt: this is not something God will do for you. It is our responsibility to get in alignment with the Word and the only way to do that is to know what the Word of God says.

The Truth of God is found in His Word, which acts as a mirror that reflects who we truly are. When we forget our true identity, we become susceptible to self-deception, entertaining thoughts and ideas that contradict reality. Many people are swayed by false beliefs and desires, which are rooted in delusion. When we allow our fleshly desires to rule us, we become trapped in a state of delusion.

Ephesians 4:22 KJV, "Strip yourself of your former nature which characterized your previous manner of life and become corrupt through lusts and desires that spring from delusion." Webster's dictionary says a delusion is "a false conviction held contrary to invalidating facts. Not factually or legally valid. Falsely reasoned." When our physical bodies and emotional states dictate our reasoning, we are susceptible to wrong thinking. However, by embracing our true identity as created by God, our desires, thoughts, and emotions transform accordingly. The Truth of God surpasses the lies propagated by Satan. We should not allow external forces such as worldly expectations or our own fleshly impulses to define us. Our true identity is only revealed by the One who calls Himself "I AM," and He alone tells us who we truly are!

Notes

Notes

_____

_____

_____

_____

_____

_____

_____

_____

_____

_____

_____

_____

_____

_____

_____

_____

_____

Notes

Notes

CHAPTER FOUR
THE WORSHIP EXCHANGE

Romans 1:21-25 KJV, "Because that when they knew GOD, they glorified him not as GOD, neither were thankful, but became vain in their imaginations, and their foolish heart was darkened. Professing themselves as wise they became fools. And changed the glory of the incorruptible GOD into an image made like corruptible man, and to birds, and four-footed beasts, and creeping things. Wherefore God also gave them up to uncleanness through the lusts of their hearts, to dishonor their own bodies between themselves. Who changed the truth of GOD into a lie and worshiped and served the creature more than the Creator who is blessed forever, Amen." Paul told the Romans here that sexual perversion is the worship of the creature rather than the Creator. You claim to be wise, but you are a fool, and your heart is in darkness.

Psalms 8:15 KJV, says concerning man "And you have crowned him with glory and honor." God, the Creator of the universe, created and gave to mankind a position of glory and honor. None had been honored by God Himself in the same way as humans, not even the angels. Humans were created in the image of God and had the privilege of having God's presence and favor within and upon them. However, through sin, humans fell short of this glory. God has never forced us to seek a close relationship with Him. Unfortunately, when man chose to sin, they lost the glory of God that was once upon them.

Glory in Hebrew is *Kavod*. It means substance, splendor, or wealth, heavy with everything good. Man was not just running around naked in the garden. Adam and Eve became aware of their nakedness following their disobedience because it instantly placed them under the rule of their flesh and senses. Prior to their disobedience, they possessed a glorified body and were wholly governed by the Spirit. Like us, they too were three-part beings consisting of a spirit, soul, and body. However, their soul and body were not in control; their spirit was in complete command. This is why we are instructed to renew our minds, subdue our bodies, and crucify our flesh.

We were meant to be clothed in the wealth of the glory of GOD. We were made to be clothed with the most expensive substance in the world and in all of creation, the glory of GOD. No other being was crowned with the honor of wearing the very rays of light, and the robes of GOD's splendor. Man will never be able to substitute the glory of GOD with the most expensive designer clothes.

Jeremiah 2:11 says "Has a nation (ever) changed gods even though they were not gods (but merely manmade objects)? But my people have exchanged their Glory

(The true GOD) for that (manmade idol) which does not benefit (them)." [AMP] Homosexuality is idolatry.

1 Timothy 4:8 AMP, says "...But godliness (spiritual training) is of value in everything and in every way, since it holds promise for the present life and for the life to come." What does profit or benefit us is to live a life of godliness. What does not profit is giving in to the sin nature we inherited from our earthly father, Adam.

Galatians 6:8 KJV, says "For he that soweth to his flesh shall of the flesh reap corruption. But he that soweth to the spirit shall of the spirit reap life everlasting."

Through the fall of man sin entered the world. And at that moment there was an exchange of the glory and light of GOD for sin and darkness. But GOD has a plan! Hebrews 2:10 KJV, says that plan is "...In bringing MANY SONS UNTO GLORY!" And that when Jesus returns in Ephesians 5:27 KJV, "That he might present to himself a <u>GLORIOUS CHURCH</u>." So, how do we get from where we are back to that position of Glory and Honor in God?

Reversing the process

First, <u>YOU MUST BE BORN AGAIN!</u>

Romans 1:21 KJV, "They <u>glorified</u> him not, neither were <u>thankful</u>..." Vs. 25 KJV, "Who exchanged the truth of GOD into a lie and <u>worshiped</u> the creature..."

Notice the use of the words 'glorified, thankful, and worshiped'. Worship is another key to living an overcoming lifestyle. The Lord told me to "reverse the process through worship and thanksgiving." Worship is setting your affections on things above and not on things on the earth. Sexual perversion is the worship of the creature because you are setting your affections on someone who does not belong to you. It is covetousness which is idolatry.

Worshiping GOD for who he is and thanking him for the Truth of GOD, which is his Word, exchanges the lie of the circumstances for the truth of his word. When we worship the creature rather than the creator, which is what homosexuality is, we exchange the truth of GOD for a lie the devil has sold. Consequently, the glory of GOD on us diminishes and turns into darkness. But, when we exchange the lie of the devil for the truth of GOD's word by worshiping the Creator, we step back into our original state of glory in GOD and the process of transformation begins. You become what you behold!

Worship is beholding the Creator. Worship, Thanksgiving, and Praise produces the glory of GOD. Psalms 119:162 KJV, says "I rejoice at thy word, as one that findeth great spoil." The truth of GOD's word is more precious than gold. How would you react if someone gave you a million dollars? That is how we need to act about God's word. We need to hold it in high esteem. Worship is the exchange of a lie for the truth, The exchange of our image into GOD's image. The more we behold him in worship, the more we become like him. The more time spent in His presence, the more we become like Him.

We were made to be changed from Glory to Glory. One of the best ways to do that is spending time in worship and fellowship with Him who created us to produce life. Worship creates an atmosphere for glory. When the glory of the Lord is manifested in us, the glory produces change.

2 Corinthians 3:18 AMP, "And we all with unveiled face continually seeing as in a mirror the glory of the Lord, are progressively being transformed into his image from (one degree of) glory to (even more) glory, which come from the Lord, (who is) the Spirit."

Exchanging the lie

Every time a thought comes, I pray "GOD, I recognize you as GOD. I honor and glorify you and give you thanks that the truth of GOD is in me. Your Word is truth. And the Word is working mightily and effectively in me who believes. Thank you that my thoughts are enlightened by your word. I rejoice at your word as one who finds great spoils. I worship you and I exchange the lie of sexual perversion for the Truth of GOD in me."

According to Philippians 2:13 KJV, "For it is GOD which all the while worketh in me both to will and to do of his good pleasure." That includes my sexual desires. I thank GOD that they are holy, they come in line with the truth. I worship GOD and thank him that his truth is in me spirit, soul, and body.

Again, Worship is *beholding* Him. You become what you behold. You behold what you see with your eyes and imagination. Worship transforms you into His image. That is what Paul meant in Romans 12:1-2 "Therefore I urge you Brothers and sisters, by the mercies of GOD, to present your bodies (dedicating all of yourselves, set apart) as a living sacrifice, holy and well pleasing to GOD which is your rational (logical, intelligent) ACT OF WORSHIP." [AMP] Paul also told us in Romans 6:13 KJV, to yield "...your members as instruments of righteousness." This is a part of worship. Yielding your thought life and your body to God is an act of worship because your body is a temple. Worship is thinking upon and speaking of our love for GOD and the acceptance of His truth and being transformed into it.

My feelings and desires must come in line with the word as I continue to thank GOD for it. And just like Abraham in Romans 4:20 KJV, I grow strong in faith as I give glory to GOD!!! I build faith in my spirit for the very thing I am thanking GOD for. Whether I see it or feel it or not. JUST LIKE ABRAHAM! God told him he was going to be the father of many nations. Yet in the natural his body was unable to perform. Romans 4:20 "But, he did not doubt or waver in unbelief concerning the promise of GOD, but he grew strong and empowered by faith, GIVING GLORY TO GOD!" AMEN!!!

This is what John 8:32 KJV, means when it says, "You shall know the truth and the truth will set you free." When you meditate on the word and worship GOD that his word is true no matter what the circumstances say. It will manifest itself in your life!

Worshiping GOD based on what he says in his word releases faith because it is acting on the word. This is what the phrase "Word of Faith" means. When faith is released, it brings change to the natural realm!

Haggai 2:9 KJV, says that "The glory of this latter house shall be greater than the former."

2 Corinthians 3:9 KJV, says "For if the ministration of condemnation be glory, MUCH MORE DOTH THE MINISTRATION OF RIGHTEOUSNESS EXCEED IN GLORY!

Thank God for his word. The word is working mightily in me. No matter what the circumstance is or what I feel or see. The word is working mightily in me! Transformation and restoration are possible to anyone no matter what sexual sin you may have committed. Sexual purity is for anyone who *believes* and *acts* on the Word.

Notes

Notes

Notes

Notes

CHAPTER FIVE

THE PRAYER LIFE OF AN OVERCOMER

Fellowship with God

When talking about a prayer life I mean a continual daily walk. Genesis 5:22 says "Enoch walked (in habitual fellowship) with God..." Vs. 24 says "And (in reverent fear and obedience) Enoch walked with God: and he was not (found among men) because GOD took him (away to be home with him)." [AMP]

My father once advised me to simply focus on being a child of God and to embrace my identity as His son, regardless of any past mistakes or shortcomings. The ultimate goal is to foster a close relationship between a father and his child, and this requires a lifestyle of continual communion with Him. By staying intimately connected with God and living in awe of Him, we invite His anointing and presence to enrich our lives.

Our hunger for God determines the level of intimacy we experience with Him. We can cultivate insight into what pleases Him through fellowship around His Word and prayer. While united prayer with others is valuable, a prayer life that is devoted solely to God is what makes united prayer truly effective. We should always be thankful for opportunities to pray with others, but it is crucial to maintain a personal prayer life with Him.

David also lived this way. Psalms 63:5-6 "My soul shall be satisfied as with marrow and fatness, and my mouth shall praise thee with joyful lips. When I remember thee upon my bed and meditate on thee in the night watches."

Psalms 101:2 KJV, "I will behave myself wisely in a perfect way. Oh, when wilt thou come unto me? I will walk within my house with a perfect heart."

Cultivating a life of prayer, praise, and fellowship with GOD in private, produces an outward, visible change that people can see. Stay close to GOD in your thoughts and in your heart. Do not allow anything to happen within you that would cost you, his presence.

King David serves as a prime example of this principle. He experienced a series of triumphs in his private life before he achieved any victories in public. This is evident in 1 Samuel 17:32-37. It seems as though the level of authority granted by God is progressive in nature. The more God can rely on us in our private lives, the more He can entrust us with the public realm. If we build a strong history with God in private, our authority will increase accordingly. As we walk in greater levels of anointing in our private lives, we can expect to experience an even greater level of anointing in public.

We need to become like Moses when it comes to the presence of GOD. Exodus 33:15-16 AMP,"And Moses said to him. "If your presence does not go (with me), do not lead us up from here. For how can it be known that your people and I have found favor in your sight? Is it not by your going with us, so that we are distinguished, your people and I, from all the (other) people on the face of the earth." Moses was about to lead the children of Israel into the promised land. It was a land flowing with milk and honey, with houses and cities that they did not build, and vineyards they did not plant. It was a land full of plenty! But Moses did not want any of it if God was not in it. If His presence did not go with them, he was willing to forfeit all of it.

We need to have this kind of tenacity about walking in the presence of GOD all day. It is His presence that sets us apart from the rest of the world. But it begins in the most private place. It is there that you practice walking in His presence. Psalms 91:1 KJV, says, "He that dwelleth in the secret place of the most High shall abide under the shadow of the Almighty." His shadow is His presence. WHEN WE INTENTIONALLY CHOOSE HIM IN PRIVATE, HE WILL INTENTIONALLY CHOOSE US IN PUBLIC!

The power and depth of my private life should surpass that of my public life. If I exhibit strength and conviction on a matter in public, it should be multiplied in private. The anointing and spiritual authority present in my private moments should exceed that of my public persona. When I address an audience, my words and actions must originate from the intimacy of my private prayer life. All my expressions must flow from that place and be a product of it.

John 15:4,5,7 KJV, "Abide in me and I in you. As the branch cannot bear fruit of itself, except it abides in the vine. No more can ye, except ye abide in me." 5" I am the vine, ye are the branches. He that abideth in me and I in him, the same bringeth forth much fruit. For without me ye can do nothing." 7 "If ye abide in me and my words abide in you, ye shall ask what ye will and it shall be done unto you."

This kind of prayer life is abiding in Him. Whatever your heart and mind revert *to* in your most private time is what you are abiding *in*. When thoughts come, instead of dwelling on it and entertaining the thought, I intentionally worship GOD instead. I bring myself into the secret place in Him that only I can stand. We all have that secret place in Christ. I bring myself into a place of intimacy with God through worship. When I find myself dwelling on the past or contemplating a decision that would separate me from his presence, I just begin to praise Him and thank Him for redeeming me from sin. I also thank him for the blood of Jesus that cleanses me and covers my thoughts, and I thank him for forgiving me and favoring me with His love. This is fellowship with Him.

Psalms 140:13 KJV, "Surely the righteous will give thanks to your name. The upright shall dwell in your presence."

Proverbs 16:6 KJV, "...by the reverent, worshipful, fear of the lord, men depart from and avoid evil."

It's important for us to grasp the true meaning of the fear of the Lord. It's a reverential awe and a deep respect for God, never wanting to displease Him. In every circumstance, we should prioritize His presence and give Him the honor He deserves. If a choice would mean losing His presence, we should choose to stay close to Him. Even in the face of temptation, we should choose to worship Him. Keeping our minds fixed on Him moment by moment will help us make Him a priority in our lives. We can show our honor and devotion to Him by allowing our thoughts and feelings to revolve around Him, and by expressing our love and gratitude to Him through our words.

Hebrews 13:15 KJV, "Through Him, therefore, let us at all times offer up to GOD a sacrifice of praise, which is the fruit of lips that thankfully acknowledge and confess and glorify His name." Hallelujah!

Putting on the new man

Another aspect of my prayer life centers on my personal growth. In every action we take, there is a side that is directed towards God and another side that is directed towards myself. This part of my prayer life is about nurturing the new creation in me by embracing my identity as a new creature in Christ. Just as we provide food and clothing for our physical bodies, we must also provide nourishment and care for our inner being.

I turn to Colossians 3:10,12, KJV, and 14 and I say "I put on the new man, which is renewed in the knowledge after the image of him who created him. I put on as God's elect, holiness, mercy, kindness, humility, meekness, longsuffering, and of these I put on love which is the bond of perfectness."

Then I turn to Ephesians 4:22,23, and 24 KJV, "I put off the old man which is corrupt according to the deceitful lusts. And I am renewed in the spirit of my mind. I put on the new man, which after GOD is created in righteous and true holiness." Here Paul says that the lusts of the flesh are deceiving.

Deception always sets in when you build your identity around the dictates of the flesh. Deception is adaptive. Meaning, evil spirits will appear from generation to generation in different clothing. The enemy uses the same old deception over and over, using different packaging.

Righteousness, holiness, forgiveness, etc, all supply power to your prayers. Like fuel to a fire. These things are wells of life or power sources to the prayer life of an overcomer.

Then I turn to Ephesians 6:10-18 KJV, and I say, "I put on the whole armor of GOD that I may be able to successfully stand up against all of the strategies and deceits of the devil." I put on......

1) <u>The helmet of salvation</u> -vs.17 a mind renewed with the word of GOD.

2) <u>Feet shod with Gospel of peace</u>- vs. 15 fully prepared to take the good news.

3) <u>The breastplate of righteousness</u>- vs. 14 confidence in knowing who you are in Christ.

4) <u>Belt of truth</u>-vs. 14 John 17:17 "Thy word is truth."

5) <u>Shield of Faith</u>- vs. 16 Belief system formed by the word of GOD.

6) <u>Sword of the Spirit</u>- vs.17 The spoken Word of God in a known tongue

7) <u>Praying in the spirit</u>- vs. 18 Praying in an unknown tongue

<u>Sharpening your sword</u>

Take note of how the helmet protects your thought life while the sword of the Spirit empowers your words and the proclamation of God's word. A sword typically has two edges, and in the spiritual realm, your two-edged sword consists of 1) your thought life and 2)

your words. If one is inconsistent with the other, your sword loses its sharpness. Alternatively, you could refer to the sword of the recreated human spirit, as "he who is joined to the Lord is one spirit with Him" (1 Corinthians 6:17) KJV.

The terms Holy Spirit and human spirit may differ, but they are sometimes used interchangeably. So, in this context, we can say that you are wielding the sword of your human spirit. To maintain a sharp edge in the spirit, keep your thoughts and words aligned with the Word of God. Confessing the Word strengthens your spirit and empowers it to rule over your soul and body. By resisting the devil, you keep your sword sharp and augment the potency of your spirit. As a result, your words carry authority supported by the power of the Word and the Blood of Jesus.

To have a sharp spirit doesn't mean being impolite. We should allow the fruits of the Spirit, such as love, gentleness, and kindness, to flow through us towards others. We should also develop self-control by consistently using the sharp sword of the Spirit against our fleshly desires and the devil. I am convinced that the primary purpose of the sword of the Spirit is to crucify our fleshly desires and take every thought captive. If we focus more on that, we will have less trouble from the devil. In Ephesians 4:27 KJV, it says, "Neither give place to the devil." We give the devil an opportunity when we fail to crucify our flesh and renew our minds.

Extended seasons of prayer

"The prayer room is God's delivery room for revival"

J. Edwinn Orr

Having established a firm foundation of consistent fellowship with GOD through prayer and embracing the new creation, I now want to address the importance of extended periods of prayer. However, it's crucial to note that such prayer sessions can only be effective if you've been continually dwelling in the secret place and putting on the new man. Once you've made it a habit, you'll never forget the profound impact of these moments of communion with GOD. You'll quickly get in tune with the Spirit, and they'll be unforgettable times with GOD. Acts 13:2 KJV, illustrates the Apostles' example of taking time to fast, worship, and pray to hear from GOD. These are the types of prayer sessions that I'm referring to.

The problem is that many people wait until these times of prayer, if they have them at all, to catch up in their prayer life. Or only worship God in church on Sunday morning. They never spend time in worship during the week in private, in their own home. But if we learn to abide in Him on a continual basis there will not be any catching up to do. Our special times of prayer will be so much further ahead, accomplished, and seasoned. We will step right into it because we are already abiding in Him.

Ephesians 6:18 KJV, "Praying always with all prayer and supplication in the Spirit..."

In 1 Corinthians 14:14-15 Paul describes praying in the spirit as praying in tongues. This is a supernatural utterance, a vocal miracle given by the Holy Spirit that you can pray aloud at will, for the purpose of devotional prayer. There is a difference between this and the public use of the gift of tongues and interpretation of tongues. However, you should desire that these gifts be manifested in your personal prayer life also.

Speaking in tongues is speaking mysteries, secret truths, and hidden things to GOD concerning His will for our lives. It is praying with your spirit man and bypassing the mind in an earthly or heavenly language unknown to you.

1 Corinthians 14:1-2 KJV

In Jude 20 it edifies and builds up the spirit man.

In 1 Corinthians 14:17 KJV, it is one way to give thanks well.

In Romans 8:26-28 KJV, we are praying the perfect will of GOD.

In 1 Corinthians 2:13 (paraphrased) we are setting forth these truths not in words taught by man's wisdom. But in words taught by the Holy Ghost!

One time in my early twenties, I had taken an extended period to pray for the will of GOD for my life. Proverbs 20:5 KJV, says, "Counsel in the heart of man is like water in a deep well, but a man of understanding draws it out."

The counsel of GOD is in us. The great counselor lives and abides in our spirits and guides us into all truth John 16:13. God's perfect will is in us and the Holy Ghost will give us counsel concerning His will by praying in the spirit.

During this season of prayer, I prayed in tongues for about an hour. I got over in the spirit. It was that place where my mind and my body were completely quiet, and I was only aware of my spirit man speaking to GOD. The phrase "in the spirit" can also mean possessed by the Holy Spirit. Suddenly, out of my mouth, the Holy Ghost spoke through me, to me. Remember I said the gift of tongues and interpretation of tongues should be operating in our devotional prayer life. 1 Corinthians 14:15 "I will pray with my spirit, and I will pray with understanding also..." The Holy Ghost spoke as I prayed in tongues, and the interpretation of it was "if you'll pray it out, you'll walk it out, and you won't have to work it out." I realized what had happened and kept saying it over and over until it rang a note of victory in my spirit. That means I prayed until there was a manifestation of joy. Such as laughing or singing.

The Holy Ghost was telling me that if I pray out the will of GOD in tongues, I will walk it out, and I would not have to work it out.

"Why is that" you may ask? Because Romans 8:28 says "GOD is working all things together for my good because I love him, and I'm called according to His purpose!" (paraphrased)

This verse is taken out of context a lot and made to say something that it is not. It does not say that GOD causes all things good and bad to happen to us for a reason. If you will read it within the context it is written. You will see that it is talking about someone who is taking hold together with the Holy Ghost against their inability to produce results (their weaknesses) and praying for the perfect plan and will of GOD. Then we can be assured and know that all things are working together for our good. And GOD is working it out when I pray it out! He will cause my steps to be ordered of Him and my will and desires to be conformed to His. <u>I will pray it out, I will walk it out, and I will not have to work it out!</u>

Another example of this happened in April of 2018. The Holy Spirit told me in prayer, through tongues and interpretation of tongues that there was coming a major shift in my family. Since 2015 when I rededicated my life to Jesus and the plan of God, I dove back into my prayer life and at the time the Holy Spirit told me that my number 1 prayer assignment at the time was my parents. I did not know what the situation was in my natural mind. I only knew I was praying them through some things. At that time, the Holy Ghost told me about a major shift coming in my family, my prayer assignment broadened to my extended family.

In July of 2018, we had a party for my Grandma Ruby's 90th birthday. A lot of my family came in from Texas, Oklahoma, and California. All the Gatlin family was there with their three boys, and their kids. At one point during the party, I knew, in my spirit, that one of the Gatlin brothers, Jason, Qwest, or Graham was moving to East Texas to start a church. My first inclination was Qwest. I even told my brother Ben in the car when we left what I sensed in my spirit. Long story short, since then, Qwest and his family moved to east Texas and we have now passed the 1st year of planting Victory City Church in Tyler, Texas.

There were also other people in the family, like my cousin Tammy, who were alerted in the spirit through dreams that something was going to happen. None of us knew what the other was sensing. All of this is a result of praying out the plan of God in the spirit. Praying in the Spirit is praying mysteries that are unknown to you that you would have otherwise never prayed in your known language.

Another major key to living the lifestyle of an overcomer is praying in tongues!

Fasting and Prayer

Acts 13:2 KJV, "As they ministered to the Lord and fasted, the Holy Ghost said...." Fasting is a crucial aspect of fellowshipping with God, but its purpose differs from that of the world's view. While some consider it as intermittent fasting for weight loss or body detox, scriptural fasting, combined with prayer, meditation on the Word, worship, and alone time with God, aims at spiritual growth. This type of fasting and prayer can move the hand of God, shift the spiritual atmosphere of a city or nation, and change the spiritual climate. In Acts 13:2, when they fasted, the Holy Spirit spoke to them. Fasting and prayer increase our sensitivity to God's voice, benefiting us, not Him. God is not withholding His Spirit or waiting for us to suffer before speaking to us. Instead, He is always speaking through the written Word (logos), the spoken Word (Rhema), or the still small voice of the Holy Spirit inside us. The question is, are we moving with Him?

If you're not experiencing personal revival, it's because you haven't chosen to engage with the Holy Ghost who is always moving. Fasting helps us become more sensitive to God's voice and enables us to move with Him. By abstaining from food for a period of time, we can quiet the voice of the flesh, which is often driven by bodily hunger, and focus on feeding our spirit instead. This is the ultimate way to crucify the flesh and its ungodly desires, as Galatians 5:24 NLT says, "Those who belong to Christ Jesus have nailed the passions and desires of their sinful nature to his cross and crucified them there." Fasting helps keep the sin nature nailed to the cross, allowing the born-again, recreated human spirit to take the driver's seat and keep the soul and body in their proper place. It heightens our spiritual senses, allowing us to see and know in the spirit without being clouded by feelings or reason. Fasting also helps to quiet the mind and maintain a disciplined thought life. When the New Creation in Christ is in charge and the flesh is under control, we become a serious threat to the kingdom of darkness.

As an example of the effectiveness of fasting and prayer, I will share my personal experience. After struggling with heavy smoking and alcohol addiction for years after rehab, I knew I needed to quit but couldn't find the strength to do so. However, during a conversation with my cousin Tammy about sobriety and addiction, she mentioned that fasting helped her quit smoking. I immediately remembered what I learned from Kenneth E. Hagin about fasting during my time at Rhema Bible School, and decided to make it a regular habit in my life.

Despite still smoking and drinking during the early weeks of fasting, I noticed that my fleshly desires were slowly diminishing, and my spirit was growing stronger. Eventually, I was able to throw away a half-empty carton of cigarettes and a bottle of whiskey without any hesitation. I continued to practice fasting and prayer regularly, and now have no desire for smoking, drinking, or any other fleshly desires, including sexual desires. Fasting and prayer has proven to be a powerful tool for keeping the desires of the flesh in check.

Matthew 6:16-18 (KJV)

16 "Moreover when ye fast, be not, as the hypocrites, of a sad countenance: for they disfigure their faces, that they may appear unto men to fast. Verily I say unto you, they have their reward.

17 But thou, when thou fastest, anoint thine head, and wash thy face;

18 That thou appear not unto men to fast, but unto thy father which is in secret: and thy father, which seeth in secret, shall reward thee openly."

Jesus explicitly warned against showing off when fasting, which is exactly what the world does when they fast for physical reasons such as weight loss or detox. They proudly flaunt their physical results, such as their weight loss and toned physique, all over social media, seeking recognition and admiration from others. However, even after their fast, they are still just as enslaved to their ungodly desires as they were before. Their flesh remains in control. Such fasting is solely for the body and serves only as a temporary, physical reward, which is precisely what Jesus cautioned against. He cautioned that if we behave this way, we will only receive a temporary physical reward, but nothing spiritually worthwhile.

Fasting spiritually reaps eternal rewards.

Galatians 5:16 says, "This I say then, walk in the Spirit, and ye shall not fulfill the lust of the flesh."

When we are more aware of the Spirit of God inside of us and we yield to Him, we will have more spiritual stamina to resist when temptation comes. Dad Hagin called this being God inside minded. Smith Wigglesworth said "Most people feed their body three hot meals a day. And feed their spirit 1 cold snack a week." Their spirit is malnourished from a lack of feeding on the Word and prayer.

Hebrews 12:1 NIV

"Therefore, seeing we also are compassed about by so great a cloud of witnesses, let us lay aside every weight, and the sin which doth so easily beset us, and let us run with patience the race that is set before us." Notice it says every weight, AND the sin. As I meditated on this topic, the Holy Spirit brought some clarity to me. I realized that there are many things in life that may not necessarily be sinful, but they still act as weights that hold us back. These things may be trivial or optional, but they can still distract us from what truly matters and hinder us from reaching our full potential. However, when we engage in scriptural fasting, we can learn to cut out the trivial and focus on the important things that will help us run our race at our maximum potential. If something is excess and we can either take it or leave it, it's best to leave it behind as it will only slow down our spiritual progress and potentially lead us to sin.

Since I have made fasting and praying a regular habit, I have shed many of the things that were weighing me down spiritually and holding me back. I have no interest in them anymore and I am now able to run my race with greater speed and focus. I plan to finish strong and get out of here running!

Ministering Spirits

The final key to living an overcoming lifestyle is often overlooked, but it's something I've personally experienced: the ministry of angels. God's Word has much to say about angels working together with us in our everyday lives and in ministry. As the return of Jesus approaches, it's important that we become more aware of their presence and learn how to cooperate with them to fulfill God's plan and purpose on earth. Let's take a look at some examples from the Word about our ministering spirits.

Hebrews 1:14 KJV, "Are they not all ministering spirits, sent forth to minister for them who shall be heirs of salvation?" Romans 8:17 KJV, says that we are "...Heirs of GOD and joint heirs with Christ." If you are Born Again, Angelic assistance is a part of your covenant with GOD. I like the way the Amplified Bible says Hebrews 1:14 "Are not all the Angels ministering Spirits sent out (by GOD) to serve (accompany, protect) those who will inherit salvation?" Of course, they are! They are sent out by GOD to serve you and me! The King James Version says "...to minister FOR THEM who shall be heirs of salvation." The Angels are there FOR US!

Psalms 91:11 says. "For He will command His Angels regarding you, to protect and defend and guard you in all your ways (of obedience and service). They will lift you up in their hands, so that you do not (even) strike your foot against a stone." [AMP]

Psalms 103:20 KJV, "Bless the Lord, you His angels, you mighty ones who do his commandments. Obeying the voice of His Word." It is crucial that we internalize these scriptures and speak them out every day, declaring God's protection over our lives. When we come across a promise in the Bible, we make it personal by confessing it out loud. As we speak God's Word, it activates His promises in our lives. His Word has the power to enforce His covenant with us, and when we declare it, we are inviting Him to work on our behalf. Therefore, let us consistently declare God's Word and allow His promises to manifest in our lives.

We know that happened to Daniel in the Old Testament. In Daniel 10:12 KJV, "Then he said to me, "Do not be afraid, Daniel, for from the first day that you set your heart on understanding this and on humbling yourself before GOD, your words were heard, and I have come in response to your words." If words spoken in faith to God could activate Angels in the Old Covenant, then in the New Covenant, it is even more powerful!

In Exodus 23:20 KJV, it says "Behold, I am going to send an Angel before you to keep and guard you on the way and to bring you to the place I have prepared."

Every day, I confess that angels are working to guide me towards the places that GOD has prepared for me, as stated in Ephesians 2:10. I also believe that I will walk in everything that GOD has ordained for me to walk in. In 2 Peter 1:3, it says that angels bring us "everything that is necessary for life and godliness."

Another important scripture that has been foundational to my personal experience with angels is Zechariah 3:7 AMP. This passage states that if we remain faithful to GOD and perform His service, we will govern His house and have charge of His courts. As a result, we will be given free access to His presence among the angels who are standing there. This means that if we are faithful with the tasks that GOD assigns us, we will see an increase in angelic activity around us, and more angels will be assigned to us.

As we remain faithful to God's calling on our lives, He entrusts us with more assignments that require greater angelic assistance. As we continue to obey and abide in His presence, we will experience an increase in spiritual authority and even be given charge over His courts, because we are speaking His Word and walking in righteousness. This will result in a constant presence of angelic activity around us, as we walk and talk where they do. The concept of courts represents authority and righteous judgment, and in the natural world, courts are where decisions are made that impact the lives, cities, and nations.

Zechariah 3:7 (MSG) "Orders from God-of-the-Angel-Armies: 'If you live the way I tell you and remain obedient in my service, then you will make the decisions around here and oversee my affairs. And all my attendants standing here will be at your service."

IF you are an Heir of salvation, this benefit is for you! The more God can trust you with small assignments, the more He can trust you with big assignments.

On Saturday evening, July 19,1997. My brother Ben Sluder and I went to my dad's church to pray. At the time he was pastoring in Tuttle, Oklahoma at Word of Faith Bible Church. We were going to have an extended time of prayer together to pray out the plan of GOD for our lives. We prayed for a while in other tongues when suddenly I was aware of someone standing behind me to the right of me. Assuming it was my brother, I opened my eyes and found myself in a three-part vision and visitation of Angels. With the first one standing right behind me. I was unaware of anything else but him. He stood as tall as the ceiling. Which happened to be about 12 feet tall. No words were exchanged. I just knew what he was there for and what I was supposed to do. He had been sent by the Father to bring Me (as well as others) into places of new graces and ability, and to open doors into new areas of ministry. And, to bring me into places in the plan of GOD that He had prepared for me. I knew I was to "LOOSE" HIM in Jesus Name. He was to take me there, but he could do nothing unless I loosed him to be able to do it on the earth. Matthew 18:18 KJV, "Whatsoever ye shall bind on earth shall be bound in heaven. Whatsoever ye shall loose on earth shall be loosed in heaven."

When he left the second one came. I knew I was to loose him regarding money and finances. Then in the third part of the vision the third Angel looked like Flames of fire! And I knew I was to loose Him on behalf of the Body of Christ as a whole, to bring them into the fullness of their place in Christ in the earth.

I happened to be reading the book Exodus when I found Ex. 23:20. I had never seen or heard that verse before and it was confirmation of what I knew to do in the vision.

In August 2001, the same angel that appeared to me in the first part of the vision in 1997, appeared to me again. In the sanctuary of New Wine Christian Center in York, PA. It was another evening of extended prayer. This time I was alone to pray out the plan. Again, it was to take me into the next place in the plan. As soon as he appeared, I was kneeling on my knees one moment, and on the floor on my back the next. He startled me. Instantly, there was an intense utterance in tongues for a period and then the interpretation. I began to pray about stepping up into the ministry on my life. And I loosed the ministering spirit to take me there. This was confirmation to a prophecy that a pastor gave me in 1998 about "stepping into new arenas of the prophetic that I have never known before and taking the church into new areas of prayer." I believe this was the same angel that held that parking space for my dad when he and Ben drove into Manhattan that day in his truck and trailer. God was taking me to new places of understanding of the anointing on my life.

But, it all happened, and I am where I am today because of spending time renewing my mind, speaking the Word, subduing my body, building a strong spirit, praying in the spirit, and loosing the ministering spirits to go before me and bring me into places GOD has prepared for me!

As overcomers, we have access into the spirit realm to bring the will of GOD into the earth through our words. Jesus gave us authority to access all the resources of Heaven including the assistance of Angels. Not only do our words subdue our body, renew our mind, and build a strong spirit man, but they also give you the ability to work with every ministering spirit at your disposal. Working with them is all about fulfilling God's will. Not ours. Speaking the promises of God in faith through words causes angelic activity. Find scriptures related to them and confess them on a regular basis.

Psalm 34:7 KJV, "The angel of the Lord encampeth round about them that fear him, and delivereth them."

Psalm 35:5-6 KJV, "Let them be as chaff before the wind: and let the angel of the Lord chase them. Let their way be dark and slippery: and let the angel of the Lord persecute them."

Psalm 68:17 KJV, "The chariots of God are twenty thousand, even thousands of angels: the Lord is among them, as in Sinai, in the holy place."

Notes

Notes

Notes

Notes

CHAPTER SIX

GRACE

More than two decades ago, when I initially began composing this book, I shared a rough draft copy with my then-pastor, Donna Ryan. Upon reading it, she advised me to add a chapter on Grace. However, I couldn't envision it at the time, as I believed I had completed the work. Soon after, I stepped down from my position and relocated to New York City. Looking back, I realize that my understanding of the grace of God was incomplete. Since then, I have undergone a significant learning process, not only testing the limits of grace but also comprehending what it truly represents and what it does not. In recent years, much has been said about grace, and there has been a significant movement in this area with remarkable teachings. However, with every truth of the Word restored to the Body of Christ, some people go too far, resulting in errors. I do not claim to know everything, and the more I learn, the more I realize how much more I must discover. Our knowledge will continue to expand as we journey through eternity in Heaven. Nonetheless, I have acquired a few insights, just scratching the surface. I intend to communicate what I do know to the best of my ability while maintaining a teachable spirit as I delve into this topic. I am always open to corrections and eager to learn more.

Greasy Grace and Messy Mercy

The concepts of grace and mercy are frequently used but often misapplied. The Bible provides extensive insights on these topics. I can use my own experience as an example. On my 40th birthday, I indulged in a trip to New York City, where my brother Ben Sluder, who resides in Ohio, came to visit and spend some time with me. During our conversation, we sat at the kitchen table of a mutual friend's apartment, gazing over Manhattan's skyline, discussing this very issue. Ben cautioned me that God was granting me a period to repent and return to the truth of God. The Age of Grace, which we are currently living in, will come to an end. My reluctance to repent constituted my decision to defy the truth and would ultimately result in ruin.

Romans 6:23 KJV, "For the wages of sin is death. But the gift of God is eternal life." Death means separation from God. Not to cease to exist. If sin separates me from God and leads to an eternity in Hell. That means being separated from everything good that comes from God. I argued with Ben that the grace of God was sufficient for me. That no matter what I did, in the end, it would all be ok. That God's grace was greater than all my sin. And it is. But I was miss interpreting that verse to say I could live any way I wanted to without any consequences and still go to heaven. That is deception. I was living by the same motto a lot of people live by these days. "Sin now, repent later" which is dangerous.

Although, there is a thread of truth in that way of thinking. 1 John 1:9 KJV says "If we confess our sins, he is faithful and just to forgive us our sins and to cleanse us from all unrighteousness." Thank God we have the assurance that if we miss it, we can always run back to God. Even after the rapture or catching away of the church during the great tribulation on the earth, God will still be giving people a chance to repent and come to the knowledge of the Truth.

But the best example of repentance is shown when temptation comes along, and instead of giving in we choose to turn and run the other way. Which is what repentance means. To change your mind, to turn and go the other way. My idea of grace at that time was like so many others. I call it greasy grace and messy mercy. Just live like the world. Any old way you want to. Even if it goes against the truth of God's word. Eventually, sin has a hefty price tag that we cannot afford to pay. The price is our life. Galatians 6:7-8 KJV, "Be not deceived. God is not mocked. For whatsoever a man soweth. That shall he also reap. For he, that sows to the flesh shall of the flesh reap corruption. But he that soweth to the spirit shall of the Spirit reap life everlasting."

Now let us apply this to sexual perversion. Jude 4 KJV, "For there are certain men crept in unawares. Who were before of old ordained to this condemnation. Ungodly men, turning the grace of God into lasciviousness. And denying the only Lord God, and our Lord Jesus Christ." Jude serves as a warning to the church, particularly regarding false teachers who promote sexual immorality and other dangerous heresies. Unfortunately, immoral teachers have been present in the church for some time. In fact, those who believe that God's plan for marriage is solely between a man and a woman are now considered the minority. Jude serves as a reminder of how God dealt with sexual sin in the past. For instance, verse 5 discusses God's response to Israel's unbelief, while verses 6-7 depict the fate of fallen angels and the corrupt Sodomites. In verses 11-13, a woe is pronounced upon such depraved teachers who advocate and endorse these behaviors.

We discussed in an earlier chapter that lasciviousness is unbridled lust and fornication. Homosexual or heterosexual. Jude is warning us that if you continue to endorse and promote sexual perversion that for you it "…is reserved the blackness of darkness forever." Jude 13b. So, grace is not the space, or breathing room, to just do whatever you want without consequences. Romans 6:14-15 KJV "For sin shall not have dominion over you. For you are not under the law, but under grace. What then, shall we sin because we are not under the law, but under grace? God forbid!"

Bethel or Beth-Aven?

As I said, the fact that there are churches, denominations, ministers, teachers, pastors, or priests who endorse sexual sin is nothing new. It goes back to the Old Testament. Hosea 5:3-4 KJV, says "I know Ephraim, and Israel is not hidden from me. Oh, Ephraim thou committest whoredom, and Israel is defiled. They will not frame their doings to turn unto their God. For the spirit of whoredoms is in the midst of them. They have not known the Lord." Now let us read this in the message translation. "I know you Ephraim, inside and out. Yes, Israel, I see right through you. Ephraim, you have played your sex and religion games long enough. All Israel is thoroughly polluted. They could not turn to God if they wanted to. Their evil life is a bad habit. Every breath they take is a whore's breath. They would not recognize God if they saw me." Ephraim is one of the 12 tribes of Israel. Whose territory was located at that time north of the tribe of Benjamin. There was a town spoken of in Joshua 7:2 and 18:12-13 KJV, called Beth-Aven that is part of a tri-city area with Ai and Bethel. Commentaries and scholars debate on the exact location (somewhere northeast of Bethel) and their proximity to each other. Bethel and Beth-Aven were probably suburbs of the larger city of Ai.

Either way, I am not here to discuss their geographical location. Beth-Aven is mentioned again in Hosea 4:15 KJV "Though thou Israel play the harlot…. Neither ye go up to Beth-Aven." And in Hosea 5:8 KJV "Blow ye the cornet in Gibeah, and the trumpet in Ramah. Cry aloud at Beth-Aven, after thee oh Benjamin." In this passage, Beth-Aven seems to be used more as a pejorative or derogatory term for Bethel instead of a reference to the actual city itself. Bethel means house of God. Beth-Aven, on the other hand, means House of idol worship. Hosea 4:16 says that Israel had backslidden because in vs 17 "Ephraim is joined to idols." And vs 18 "They have committed whoredom continually." In those days pagans worshiped their idols and false gods through sexual activity and temple prostitution.

Israel and its Aaronic and Levitical priests left their holy priesthood duties of offering sacrifices in the temple of the Lord, to go "worship" pagan gods through sex. In 2 Chronicles 31:1 it says that under king Hezekiah's reign, these high places and altars of pagan worship were all throughout Ephraim, and Benjamin, and all of Israel. Thankfully, Hezekiah did that which was right in the sight of the Lord and threw down the places of idol worship until they were utterly destroyed, 2 Chronicles 29:2.

The question I want to ask you is this. Are you a Bethel, or a Beth-Aven? A house of the living God, or a house of idol worship? In 2 Chronicles 13:4 the prophet "Abijah stood up... and said hear me thou Jeroboam and all Israel." Vs 8b-9 "there are with you golden calves which Jeroboam made for you for gods. Have ye not cast out the priests of the Lord, the sons of Aaron and the Levites, and have made you priests after the manner of the nations of other lands? So that whosoever cometh to consecrate himself with a young bullock and seven rams, the same may be a priest of them that are no gods."

If Abijah were alive today, he would be calling out the churches and religions that are ordaining openly homosexual priests. Telling them they are in idolatry. Worshiping the creature, rather than the creator. 2 Chronicles 13:20 KJV, says that "Neither did Jeroboam recover his strength again in the days of Abijah. And the Lord struck him, and he died." Vs 21 "But Abijah waxed mighty" Jeroboam was from the tribe of Ephraim! And he was promised great blessings if he would only follow the Lord. Abijah eventually did do much evil in God's sight and only ruled in Judah for three years. When Abijah died his son Asa reigned. Asa instituted reform and removed the temple prostitution in 2 Chronicles 14:2-4 "And Asa did that which was good in the sight of the Lord his God for he took away the altars of the strange gods. And the high places and break down the images and cut the groves. And commanded Judah to seek the Lord God of their fathers. And to do the law and the commandments." All these Old Testament accounts go to show you that just like the church today, ungodly men and women were turning the Grace of our God into lasciviousness.

Sexual perversion crept into the "pulpit" then just as it is now. And I am calling it out for what it is. And just like the prophet in Hosea 6:1 KJV, I am proclaiming to you "come and let us return to the Lord!"

Instruments of Righteousness

In Ezra 6:5 King Darius made a decree. "And also let the golden and silver vessels of the house of God (Bethel) which Nebuchadnezzar took forth out of the temple, which is at Jerusalem, take everyone to his place, and place them in the house of God."

Apostle Paul says to the church at Corinth in 1 Corinthians 6:15-19 KJV, "Know ye not that your bodies are members of Christ? Shall I take the members of Christ and make them members of a harlot? God forbid. What, know ye not that which is joined with a harlot is one body? For two, saith he, shall become one flesh. But he that is joined to the Lord is one spirit. Flee fornication… What know ye not that your body is the temple of the Holy Ghost, which is in you, which ye have of God, and ye are not your own."

2 Corinthians 6:16 KJV, "And what agreement hath the temple of God with idols? For ye are the Temple of the Living God…" Romans 6: 12-13 KJV,"Let not sin therefore reign in your mortal body, that you should obey it in the lusts thereof. Neither yield ye your members as instruments of unrighteousness unto sin. But yield yourselves unto God, as those who are alive from the dead. And your members as instruments of righteousness to God." Our physical bodies do not belong to us. My body - my choice is deception. Our body belongs to God. 1 Corinthians 6:20 "…therefore glorify God in your body and your spirits, which are God's."

As a born-again believer, the Holy Spirit resides within you, and you are united with Christ in spirit. You are a Bethel, a dwelling place of God. However, when we submit to sexual sin, our bodies become

Beth-Aven, a dwelling place for idol worship. Sexual immorality is a "work of the flesh," which occurs when we succumb to our fleshly desires and let them take control, as mentioned in Galatians 5:19-21. It is also considered idolatry, as sexual activity outside of God's design is a form of worshiping something other than God, as stated in 2 Corinthians 6:17: "Therefore, come out from their midst and be separate," says the Lord. "And do not touch what is unclean."

Divine Influence

Let's revisit Romans 6:14 which in the KJV states, "For sin shall not have dominion over you: for ye are not under the law, but under grace." I believe the key to understanding and practicing Romans 6:12-13 is found in verse 14. In the original Greek, the word "grace" is used in various ways. According to the Strong's Concordance, 5485, 5486 - Charis - it can be defined as graciousness of action or manner, something that is acceptable, a benefit, favor, gift, liberality, joy, pleasure, or something worthy of thanks. However, I want to focus on one particular definition - the divine influence upon the heart and its reflection in life.

The concepts of God's unmerited favor, graciousness in salvation, and liberality of love are often discussed, but the idea of divine influence on the heart is not emphasized as much. When we accept Jesus as our savior, we are responding to this divine influence.

In Ephesians 2:8, the phrase "by grace" refers to this divine influence on the heart, while the phrase "saved through faith" describes its reflection in our lives. In Romans 5:17, 20, and 21, the phrases "abundance of grace," "where grace did much more abound," and "even so might grace reign through righteousness" all refer to God's divine influence on the heart, with the phrase "unto eternal life by Jesus Christ our Lord" reflecting its impact in our lives. When I encounter the word "grace," I now think of it as representing the reality that no one under the law could keep it perfectly, and that the law was given to reveal our need for a savior.

And we are still not perfect. However, the difference between then and now is that the blood of Jesus has made atonement for our sins. He is the spotless Lamb of God. Without sin. When we make him the Lord of our life, we have an unlimited supply of divine influence living inside of us through God the Holy Spirit. Now, we need to do what 2 Peter 3:18 says KJV "But grow in grace and in the knowledge of our Lord and Savior Jesus Christ." The Christian walk is a process of spiritual growth in that divine influence, or grace. And learning how to draw on it from our born-again recreated human spirits.

Abundance of Grace

The key to growing in the grace of God and yielding to His divine influence is in the same verse. 2 Peter 3:18 KJV, "...and in the knowledge of our Lord and savior Jesus Christ." John 1:1 KJV, says "In the beginning was the Word, and the Word was with God, and the Word was God." If you want to grow in the knowledge of Jesus, spend time in the Word! Spend time meditating on the Word and renewing your mind with it. Building a strong spirit with it. If you want to get to know someone, spend quality time with them. The more you fellowship with Him around His Word, the more you get to know Him. As you grow in your understanding of grace, the divine influence upon your heart becomes stronger, and its reflection becomes more apparent in your life. This principle applies to all relationships: the more time you spend with someone, the greater their influence on you. In Philippians 2:13, Paul refers to this dynamic when he states that "it is God who works in you both to will and to do of His good pleasure." This points to the divine influence that shapes your heart and manifests in your actions.

Colossians 1:29 AMP "For this I labor unto weariness, striving with all the superhuman energy which HE SO MIGHTILY ENKINDLES AND WORKS IN ME."

Hebrews 13:21 KJV, "Now may the God of peace... make you perfect in every good work to do His will. Working in you that which is well pleasing in His sight through Jesus Christ." These verses all speak of divine influence. Growing in the Grace of God happens when "the Word of God effectually worketh in you that believe."

1 Thessalonians 2:13 KJV, When the word is working effectively and mightily in us then we are growing in grace! And the more we grow in grace, that divine influence becomes something called Charisma. The Greek meaning of it is a divine gratuity, deliverance from danger or passion, a spiritual endowment or religious qualification, a miraculous faculty, or a gift. I love all of it. But the part I love the most is where it says spiritual endowment or qualification. The same word charisma is used in 1 Corinthians 12:1 KJV, "Now concerning spiritual gifts..." In the original Greek it only said spirituals. Meaning things of or pertaining to the Holy Spirit. Charis is the divine influence of God on our heart. Charisma is the reflection of it in our life. As we grow in the grace of God Charisma begins to operate.

As we grow in grace, the result will be the manifestation of the fruit of the Spirit in our lives. The gifts of the Spirit listed in 1 Corinthians 12 are intended to empower us, while the fruit of the Spirit described in Galatians 5:22-23 is meant to shape our character. It is our character that will keep us on the right path and enable us to continue to operate in the power of the Spirit.

No character, no Charis, no Charisma, NO COURSE. To remain on track with God's plan for our lives, we require His grace, but our own actions are also essential. In the kingdom of God, every aspect has a divine and human dimension. We must collaborate with God by immersing ourselves in prayer and the Word of God, as well as by practicing the principles presented in this book. It is impossible to lead an aimless life without regular fellowship with God and expect to grow in His grace. As with any relationship, spending more time with the one you love increases their influence on you and rubs off on you. Amen!

Notes

Notes

Notes

Notes

CHAPTER SEVEN

A CALL TO ACTION

Change your Confession

In the first section of this chapter, I want to address the church and those who have loved ones that have been deceived by the enemy and are not walking in the truth. My immediate family and close relatives, who were aware of the calling God had on my life, never aligned themselves with the world by referring to me with the labels the world used. They recognized that my sinful nature was not the real me, and that the true Steven had a divine purpose. They knew this from the time I was a young child and never wavered, standing firmly on the Word of God and claiming His promises for my life, even in the midst of seemingly hopeless situations. In contrast, I have encountered numerous well-meaning Christians who agree with the world's opinions rather than aligning themselves with what God's Word declares. 2 Corinthians 5:18 teaches us that we have been entrusted with the ministry of reconciliation.

A part of our priestly role in Christ, 1 Peter 2:5,9, is to say the same thing that God says. In Hebrews 3:1 Jesus is called the HIGH PRIEST of our profession or confession. Homologeo is the Greek word for confession, and it means to "say the same thing." The power of agreement works both ways. If the devil can get you to agree with what he says about them instead of agreeing with the Word, he can hinder progress. We need to HOMOLOGEO what our high priest Jesus says by speaking the Word over them. As we begin to confess, agree, or say the same thing God says circumstances must change. Start acting like the Word is true in their lives. Begin daily speaking aloud with your mouth and thanking Him that the Scriptures are true. Make the promises of God about them a part of your everyday life. When God's words become your words, they will cause you to walk in victory over any circumstance. It is through your meditation and confession of the Word of God concerning that loved one that will bring them through.

An incredible illustration of this principle occurred when I was in my early twenties. After completing high school, I enrolled at Rhema Bible College but did not complete my first year. Subsequently, I moved back in with my parents in Tuttle, Oklahoma, where they pastored Word of Faith Bible Church. Eventually, I moved to Oklahoma City, and for lengthy periods, my family had no idea where I was living or how to contact me. During this time, I spent my nights hopping from one bar to another, clubbing, and engaging in promiscuous behavior. The only time I would visit my family was during holidays, and I always arrived unannounced, showing up late and leaving early. My family would not see or hear from me for long stretches of time. Although they were pleased to see me, I always brought a sense of heaviness with me. On one occasion, I returned home for Thanksgiving, but I remained cold and bitter toward my family. When I left, there was an air of sadness, a gloomy and depressing feeling about my situation, and the fact that no one knew where I was going or how to reach me weighed heavily on my family. After I left, there was silence for a while. However, my father and brother looked at each other and exchanged a small smile.

The grins soon turned into chuckles. This went on for a while. And after a few minutes, the chuckles turned into all out Holy Ghost belly laughter which was contagious and spread to my mom and sister. Before they knew it, they were all laughing so hard they were weeping and wiping away the tears. The power of God fell in the house that evening and they began to rejoice and shout the victory in faith. They carried on like this in the spirit for an hour or more. The spirit of heaviness I left behind lifted, and they had a Holy Ghost meeting right there at home. Dad Hagin used to call it an east Texas brush arbor spell. That is shouting, crying, dancing, and running all at once. Dad Hagin taught us to laugh at the devil. We had many services like this in church. In our circles, we believe in being drunk in the spirit. But this did not happen in church. It started in the kitchen and made its way to the living room. They passed up an excellent opportunity to be depressed and down in the mouth. They could have easily let themselves make the wrong confession. But what were they doing!? Psalm 119:162 NLT says, "I rejoice in your Word like one who discovers great treasure." They were rejoicing at what they knew God's Word said about me. Instead of agreeing with the devil, they were laughing at the devil because God's Word is true, and the devil is a liar. They knew Psalm 2:4 said, "He who sits in the heavens laughs."

They knew they were seated in heavenly places in Christ Jesus, Ephesians 2:6. They knew they were drawing from the wells of salvation with joy like Isaiah 12:3 says. Instead of dealing with the situation out of fear and despair they were dealing with it in Faith because faith shouts before the walls come down. It shouts before it sees the answer and laughs in the face of defeat. They refused to say anything other than what God said about me and acted like it was true!

Around that same time, I went to visit my family unexpectedly after a night of partying in Oklahoma City. I fell asleep while driving on a major highway and crashed my car into oncoming traffic, completely totaling it. Fortunately, no one else was injured. My parents were called to the scene and I was rushed to the hospital, but miraculously, I only had a few bruises. At the same time, my sister ReJeanna was traveling with the Kenneth E. Hagin crusade team and felt prompted to pray in the spirit for someone in our family. She didn't know who at the time, but later found out about my accident from our mother. This is an excellent example of being led by the Holy Spirit to pray for your family, as mentioned in Romans 8:26, where the Holy Spirit comes to our aid and helps us pray according to the perfect will of God.

My grandmother Ruby Eastwood who was a Pentecostal Holiness preacher and pastor my whole life had prayer most every weekday morning back when she Pastored, which was over 50 years. She created a pattern of prayer for her children, grandchildren and so many others to follow.

Those years that I was running from God and His call on my life, grandma would call my cousin Tammy to meet with her to pray for me many times. She knew to set her whole morning aside because they would be praying for hours. Grandma's prayers were different than other Christians we knew. When she started out to pray, she made up her mind to pray for the thing all the way through to victory. She did not pray too much in English, just enough to know they were headed in for spiritual warfare on behalf of my soul.

She would pray so deeply that she was groaning utterances with the help of The Holy Ghost. She would start out crying before God and she would end up laughing and rejoicing that it was done! We learned so much from those many years of praying with Grandma. There was absolutely no doubt that it was only a matter of time before I would come home just like the prodigal son. Tammy remembers clearly as the family would gather; someone would ask about me. Her answer was always the same. Never wavering. Always declaring and decreeing the victory that would establish my future in Christ.

My brother Ben also had an amazing experience with Grandma in prayer. The summer after his first year at ORU he took a trip to California to visit Grandma Ruby and the rest of the family. While he was there, he was able to schedule some preaching engagements at a few churches. One place he wanted to visit was Morrow Bay. This day was something special. Let us say it was a divine appointment, because Ben never had the opportunity to just sit and really get to know Grandma Ruby like he did that day, driving back home to Bakersfield from Morrow Bay.

He had developed a love for Bible Prophecy, and he wanted to know what Grandma Ruby thought about the end times, where we were in the timeline. She blew his mind on how much she had studied this subject. She was a student. She had to be to preach from a place of power. Not only was she a student, but she was a pray-er. Growing up we learned that at any given moment, no matter where we were, she was known to touch heaven with her cry of faith.

Every person in her family was affected by her prayers. That day, on their way back to Bakersfield, from Morrow Bay. Grandma took ahold of his hand, while driving, and said, "Ben, we need to pray for Steven!" There was urgency in her voice as she said it. There was no doubt. There was only faith. He understood this was something she did on a regular basis, was to lift her voice to the God of heaven to make a petition for her family members. That day I was in her heart. This was an experience in prayer Ben would never forget. Grandma would pour her heart out for me, and so did Ben, for the next hour or so, praying in a heavenly language that only God the Holy Spirit could give us to petition the throne of Yahweh. She set an example for us to follow in that car. She laid out a template for prayer. Someone said before that the spirit of prayer is better caught than taught. That day Ben caught it, and my siblings and I, including others in my family, will go to that place, to pray for those in need. We are a family of pray-ers. We are people of faith. It is our mission and our calling.

There should be mockers

Jude 17-20 KJV, "But, beloved, remember ye the words which were spoken before of the apostles of our Lord Jesus Christ. How that they told you there should be mockers in the last time, who should walk after their own ungodly lusts. These be they who separate themselves, sensual, having not the Spirit. But ye beloved, building up yourselves on your most holy faith praying in the Holy Ghost." Jesus said that in the last days the world would become much like the days of Noah. Matthew 24:37 KJV, "But as the days of Noah were, so shall also the coming of the Son of man be."

We may not know the exact day or hour, but we can recognize the signs of the times and seasons through the many prophecies in the Bible. Sadly, many people ignore or avoid Bible prophecy, which makes up almost two-thirds of the Bible. Jesus warned us about the prevalence of deception before his second coming, urging us to be vigilant and not to be misled. In fact, deception was the first thing he mentioned in Matthew 24:4. The people during Noah's time were also living in disbelief, just like many today. Noah preached a message of repentance and warned of coming judgment on sin for 140 years, but he was mocked and ridiculed. However, he knew he had heard from God and urged people to get into the ark. Today, the "ark" is Jesus Christ. We need to seek refuge in him before it's too late. The door is slowly closing, and we are approaching the end of the age of grace.

The Right Side of History

During a past presidential election, when there were two prominent candidates, someone told me that they were voting for a certain candidate because they were "on the right side of history." That statement stayed with me, and I began to reflect on it in light of the Bible's teachings about our current times and prophecy. The return of Jesus Christ and our rapture to be with him are incredibly close. As 1 Corinthians 15:52 KJV, states, "in a moment, in the twinkling of an eye, at the last trumpet: for the trumpet shall sound, and the dead shall be raised incorruptible, and we shall be changed."

This event we call the rapture will usher in a period called the great tribulation. Revelation 9:20-21 "The rest of mankind who were not killed by these plagues still did not repent of the work of their hands; they did not stop worshiping demons, and idols of gold, silver, bronze, stone, and wood—idols that cannot see, hear, or walk. 21 Nor did they repent of their murders, their magic arts, their sexual immorality, or their thefts." This passage of scripture reveals that there will be people left behind after the rapture of the church who did not repent of sexual immorality among many other things. In other words, because of their lack of repentance they found themselves on the wrong side of history. I thought about this the day I heard that statement. I do not know about you, but I want to find myself on the right side of history when Jesus comes. A Bible prophecy teacher that I follow heavily, Amir Tsarfati said this. "The decisions you make today will determine whether you are a heaven dweller or an earth dweller when Jesus comes." I intend on being a heaven dweller and finding myself on the right side of history! Remember we said that repentance means to change your mind to turn and walk the other way.

The Lord's Side

Exodus 32:26 KJV

"Then Moses stood in the gate of the camp, and said, who is on the LORD'S side? Let him come unto me. And all the sons of Levi gathered themselves together unto him." When Moses came down from the mountain and found the Israelites worshiping a golden calf, he drew a line with them. By saying this, he meant that their idolatry was wrong. They had left the worship of the one true God to worship an idol made with hands. He was saying that if they did not get back on the Lord's side there would be profound consequences.

God's Word is God's will.

God's side is the right side of history. Revelation 16:9-11 KJV says "...and they repented not to give Him glory. And repented not of their deeds."

Revelation 21:8 KJV says "But the fearful, and unbelieving, and the abominable, and murderers, and whoremongers, and sorcerers, and idolaters, and all liars, shall have their part in the lake which burneth with fire and brimstone: which is the second death." Chapter

2:22 "And I gave her (jezebel) the space to repent of her fornication, and she repented not…. Except they repent of their deeds." We said in the chapter on grace that it is not the space to do whatever we want without consequences. Grace is the space God is giving us to repent. To come back to the Truth of God and the truth of His Word. We need a great awakening to the Truth of God! Not a "woke" kind of awakening to your truth and my truth. Wake up to the Truth of God!

Repentance

2 Corinthians 7:10

Amplified Bible

"For [godly] sorrow that is in accord with *the will of* God produces a repentance without regret, *leading* to salvation; but worldly sorrow [the hopeless sorrow of those who do not believe] produces death."

There are two types of repentance: godly sorrow that leads to a true change of heart and direction, and worldly sorrow that is only sorry for getting caught and will repeat the same mistake. Exodus 9:27-35 gives an example of worldly sorrow when Pharaoh confessed his sin during the plagues in Egypt but did not truly fear God or turn away from his sin. Instead, he sinned more and hardened his heart. Most people repent like Pharaoh, saying sorry but continuing their old ways, which leads to destruction and death. God will give people time to repent, but eventually, His hands will be tied and there will be no more spare time.

A perfect example of true repentance is chapter Psalm 51. Read the entire chapter on your own. It is a prayer of repentance King David prayed. In which are found the famous words "create in me a clean heart, O God: and renew a right spirit within me." Vs 10. David was an adulterer and a murderer. When he confessed his sin before God and asked for forgiveness, he did it with a broken spirit. That means he humbled himself before God with a complete feeling of remorse.

To repent, we must acknowledge our sins and accept Jesus' sacrifice for them. We must trust in His grace, which empowers us to turn away from our old ways with the help of the Bible and the Holy Spirit. According to 2 Corinthians 7:10, this kind of repentance will not be regretted. In Ezekiel 18:30b, 32, God urges us to turn away from our transgressions and avoid eternal separation from Him. He takes no pleasure in the death of the wicked. In 2 Thessalonians 2:10, we learn that those who perish do so because they did not accept the truth. God desires all to be saved, as 1 Timothy 2:4 tells us. We should continually turn our hearts and minds to Him and aim to grow in grace, confessing our sins immediately. We should strive for a lifestyle of repentance, not perfection.

We should also take a good look at what happened to Jonah and the city of Nineveh. God called him to preach repentance to them. Although initially he said "No" and ran the other way to Tarshish. We know the story that eventually he did go to Nineveh and in Jonah 3:5, 10 KJV it says, "so the people of Nineveh believed God... and God saw their works that they turned from their evil way." And there was great repentance in that city and a great deliverance from destruction. Because of Jonah's obedience an entire city was saved and turned to God! I am looking for entire cities and nations to repent and wake up to the truth!

You can be set free from any sexual sin that you are struggling with. Don't be like those mentioned in Jude 18 and 19 who ridicule God's word and the possibility of freedom from sexual sin. God has provided paths for us to follow that lead to a satisfying and fulfilling life. Along these paths, there are relationships and connections that provide us with the necessary tools to get us to where we need to be. This book is a manifestation of my prayer life and my time spent alone with God. I believe it has infused you with faith and truth, enabling you to progress to the next level of growth and freedom from any sexual bondage or addiction that may be holding you back. The Word of God is shedding light on these matters so that we can break free from unhealthy habits and addictive behaviors. By embracing the truths in this book, derived from God's Word, and incorporating them into your daily life, you can walk in His presence, worship Him, and pray. Take it one step at a time and allow God to guide you towards the freedom He has promised. YOU WILL WALK IN VICTORY OVER ANY AND EVERY SEXUAL SIN that might have a hold of you.

Revelation 3:19 KJV

"Be zealous therefore and repent."

Luke 24:47 NKJV

"And that repentance and remission of sins should be preached in His name to all nations, beginning at Jerusalem."

Acts 17:28-31 KJV

"To open their eyes and to turn them from darkness to light. From the power of Satan unto God. That they may receive forgiveness of sins."

1 Timothy 2:4-5 KJV

"Who will have all men to be saved and come to the knowledge of the truth. For there is one God and one mediator between God and man, the man Jesus Christ."

2 Peter 3:9 KJV says that God is "...not willing that any should perish but that all should come to repentance."

Acts 3:19 KJV

"Repent ye therefore and be converted that your sins may be blotted out..."

Acts 4:12 KJV

"Neither is there salvation in any other, for there is none other name under Heaven given among man whereby we must be saved."

Prayer of salvation

Psalm 32:1,5 KJV says "Blessed is he who…is forgiven. I acknowledge my sin unto thee…I will confess."

John 3:3 KJV, "…except a man be born again, he cannot see the kingdom of God."

Romans 10:9 "That if thou shalt confess with thy mouth the Lord Jesus and shalt believe in thine heart that God hath raised Him from the dead, thou shalt be saved." KJV

Do not be a mocker and get left outside of the ark. Get on the right side of history. The Lord's side. Pray this prayer with me. "Lord Jesus I am a sinner. I need a Savior. I confess the sin of homosexuality. And all my sins. Wash me with the Blood of Jesus and make me clean. I confess that you are my Lord and God raised you from the dead and I am saved. I am born again. I am now a new creation in Christ. Old things have passed away. All things have become new. Eternal salvation is my inheritance.

And I AM SAVED. AMEN!"

As a child of God, you have the power to control your body, renew your mind, and sharpen your spiritual sword. You are not just a conqueror but an overcomer. Live your life as a ruler, not subject to circumstances. Believe that transformation is possible and that you can achieve victory over the flesh. Hold onto God's Word and keep it in your thoughts, words, and actions. My sister, ReJeanna, once told me, "Steven, it's all about the Word, the Word, the Word!" Never give up, because this is the life of an overcomer. We will run our race and finish our course with joy!!!!!!!!!!! Bringing many sons unto glory!

Notes

Notes

Notes

Notes

CHAPTER EIGHT

A message to parents: Paul and Janet Sluder

"Train up a child in the way he should go and when he is old he will not depart from it." Proverbs 22:6 KJV.

We were blessed to have three healthy children. Steven is our first born with a loving, happy disposition. He loved to sing. He was the sensitive one on the playground, as told by his kindergarten teacher, to care for others if they were hurt.

From the time our kids were born we taught the word of God to each child. In school we memorized a monthly chapter together. We made it a priority as a family to quote scripture from memory before leaving the supper table. We felt it was our obligation to keep them in church and teach them about Jesus and his word at home. It was important to us for them to be in a Christian school. So Janet worked at the school to pay their tuition.

Every child has different strengths and they can be sought out and developed. Steven sang with different groups at school and in church. At 15 he preached his first message and the word of God rolled out of him for 45 minutes. One day when he was 13, I was spending a relaxing evening at home after a hard day's work of hanging drywall. The very last thing on my list of things to happen in life, happened.

Steven, the oldest of my three perfect children, came to me and said that he needed to talk to me in private. We entered my bedroom and sat on the floor across from each other with legs crossed like a couple of Indians about to smoke a peace pipe. What came out his mouth next was something completely unexpected and very gut wrenching. He began to tell me about some sexual encounters he was having. As he spoke, my mind was spinning. I could not believe what my ears were hearing. I was angry and overwhelmed with emotion.

This happened during a time when many young men were beginning to "come out of the closet" about their homosexuality and suffered rejection from their parents and others because of the way they reacted from their emotions. Only to drive them further and deeper into a perverted lifestyle. While he talked I was thinking about how I was going to respond and what I should say. Something in me said to "just listen." So, I just listened. I decided that it was better to respond out of my love for him and keep the lines of communication open.

I asked a few questions along the way and listened some more. Once it was clear that he had gotten everything off his chest I read some scriptures from the Bible about the issue and we prayed and asked God for forgiveness. It is always about the sin, never about the person. We also decided that we would seek help from the counseling resources in our local church.

The road going forward was rocky for a while with a few more encounters but then we saw a change for the better which lasted for the better part of his teen years. Steven developed good solid relationships with other dedicated believers and especially people with strong prayer lives. Some of which became mentors and influencers in his life long into his adulthood.

During his high school years, Steven became strong spiritually and God began to use him in some outstanding ways. All night prayer meetings, developing the first ever bible club in his high school, and confronting witchcraft within the teaching staff of his high school. Both on the spiritual level and outright face-to-face. I have always loved my son more than words could tell, through the good and the bad. But during this season I was especially proud of him.

Before I give you the impression that the battle was over at that point, and I begin to offer words of encouragement that might help you in your struggles, let me tell you that for the next 20 plus years the powers of hell were unleashed upon that young man's soul in ways we could not have imagined. I won't go into details. But as his parents we had many gut wrenching and heartbreaking moments. He almost lost his life and his mind because of the drug abuse and illicit lifestyle he was living.

It has been a slow, steady progress over the years but today Steven is living an addiction free life in Christ and has been consistently growing stronger in the Lord. However, the fight is not over and will not be until one day we put off mortality and put on immortality. Put off corruption and put on incorruption. The difference in our fight now is in the fact that we no longer fighting from a place of crisis to crisis but from a place of victory in Christ. No longer from a defensive position but from a position of offense by daily putting on the armor of God and staying in close intimate fellowship with Him. In the natural there were times that it seemed hopeless. If it had not been for the word of God and the power of the Holy Spirit, it certainly would have been. But because we were already anchored in the Word, knowing His promises, how faith works, and past miracles we experienced in our own lives, we knew there was hope.

God was, is, and always will be our hope and our salvation. Our victory can be your victory too because our victory is in God. Remember that no matter what happens demonstrate love. Even in your tough side. There are times when you must remain firm and apply discipline but never from a place of anger. And never ever make your child the issue. It is never about the child. It is always about the sin. When the opportunity presents itself, point him or her to the truth in the word of God in a non-judgmental way, and lead them to repentance.

Keep the lines of communication open by being a good listener regardless of how shocked you might be at what your child says. Believe me when I say I heard some shocking things. A lot of "TMI" from my thirteen year old child. And you will too if you haven't already. Your situation may be completely different from ours. In fact, your "child" may already be an adult. but these principles still apply.

Steven and I have always been able to talk about anything. Because of these simple truths. Just be a good listener and respond in kindness. If you are going to enter spiritual combat for the life and the soul of your child, realize that this is a spiritual warfare that must be fought with spiritual weapons. Not a physical one. There are many resources and tools available to help you in your fight. But your best weapon is the word of God and if it is not based on what God says, trash it.

Renew your mind with what God's word says about your child, think what God says, speak what God says about him or her. That is what faith does, that's how faith operates and gets things done. Faith sees the unseen and calls things that are not as though they were. Steven's mother and I refused to call him a Homosexual.

Our confession is that he is created in the image and likeness of God, he is a new creature in Christ, old things are passed away and all things are new, he is the righteousness of God in Christ, he is called and anointed by the Holy Ghost and wherever he goes the presence of God goes with him. He is created for

God's pleasure and will fulfill the plan and purpose of God for His life. Keep God's word coming out of your mouth. It is powerful and effective. Never give in to the pressure of popular culture, social norms, and ideology about your child. Never call them what the world calls them. God's word is final authority!

You have read about how heartbreaking this was for his mom and me, we both dealt with bouts of depression. But God's wonderful promises always brought us out of it. The word will also guard your heart and mind from discouragement and depression and bring you tremendous supernatural joy. When you know the Word of God you know that there is no way the devil can win this fight because he has already been defeated. No matter how hard he tries. Jesus made toast out of him 2000 years ago.

The joy of the lord contains supernatural strength and it is also one of the fruits of the Spirit listed in the book of Galatians. For example, there was this one time when the family had gathered for thanksgiving. We enjoyed our dinner and had an enjoyable time of fellowship with each other. After a brief time, Steven said his goodbyes and left. This was during one of those rocky times where things were not going well and we had not seen him in a while. Upon his leaving there was a heaviness that we all felt. It was unspoken, but it was in the air. My youngest child Benjamin and I briefly looked at one another and we could see it in each other's eyes. But suddenly a small grin appeared on our faces, our eyes lit up, and our small grin turned into a chuckle as if to say "yes," I know what you are thinking. The devil is defeated and does not stand a chance, because we knew what the word said about the situation. Our chuckle turned into laughter as we made our way into the living room where My wife Janet and my daughter ReJeanna were. Benjamin and I continued laughing and it spread to Janet and

ReJeanna. Which then turned into a wildly hilarious, supernatural laughing session that lasted close to an hour. We all had a sense that a supernatural breakthrough had happened that night in the spirit.

Let the joy of the Lord be your strength. Nehemiah 8:10

Cousin Tammy's Dream

In the dream I was on my way to this castle. The castle was so big that from where I was standing, there was no way I could see all of it.

As I made my way around the side of the castle, I came upon a tower that was very tall. I walked in through the door and wound up at the stairway. At the very top of the tower, I came to another door. I do not know how, but I knew this place belonged to Steven. I knocked on the door. As the door was opened and I was welcomed in by the sweetest elderly couple who were servants there. They were the most amazing people and so young looking for their age. As I began to look around, I was captivated by the appearance of his home. Every detail was in place. Though Steven had not arrived there yet, this couple knew he was coming and kept everything prepared for his arrival. They had a banqueting table spread with a feast that one can only dream about.

Everything there had one purpose and that was to be ready for Steven's arrival. There were high expectations for what was about to come.

Cristie Frederick's Dream

This dream took place on Sunday, August 26, 2001. Cristie Frederick was a member of New Wine Christian Center in Wrightsville, Pennsylvania. Where I took the position of music director for Pastors Barry and Donna Ryan. It was lost by me along with my old prayer journals after I left New Wine and moved to Manhattan. It was recently rediscovered and found in storage on June 11, 2022. It was in a sealed envelope that had never been opened or read by me until now, 22 years later. For such a time as this.

Notice some similarities between this and Tammy's dream.

"There was a small one-story house set apart on NWCC's property. It was elevated on a mound. Like a mote or an island in the middle of a flat field. It was a little white house with brown shutters, a brown roof, with flowers planted all around and in window boxes. Roseanne Kendig took me inside the house and showed me around. The dining room was nicely furnished. It was there that Roseanne told me the church owned the house and had furnished it. We were currently letting Steven Sluder live there. Just then, Steven walked in and asked if we wanted to see the rest of the house. He was taking his clean white laundry upstairs, so he showed us his bedroom. Which was a small room on the second level. The only room above the first floor of the house. Steven was incredibly pleased about the arrangement and had a big smile on his face that made his countenance glow. Roseanne mentioned that the house cost $186,000.00. I was incredulous at the price of such a small home." Then she writes the interpretation of the dream using the book "Understanding the dreams you dream," by Ira Milligan (Treasure House)

Interpretation

Your gifting in praise and worship has made room for you at NWCC where the leadership has placed you in a position of authority. It is here where the Lord will use you as an instrument of change or a new move into prophetic praise and worship. The Lord knows your passion is for Him, and that you strive to live in righteousness. His purpose in this time will be accomplished as you spend much time alone with Him in worship. Allowing the Holy Spirit to teach you how to move in the prophetic so that you may lead the worship team and congregation in it as well. This swift maturity may come as a surprise to others. And will call for wisdom on your part for this new level which will bring you much joy.

New House: New life, change, revival, new move.

Roseanne Kendig: Church elder, spiritual authority, mother figure. Love, kindness. I lived with James and Roseanne for a couple of months when I moved to Pa until I found my own place. I became close to them and their family. Roseanne is a strong intercessor. We had MANY great times in prayer together. I slept in the guest room upstairs and was often woken up early in the morning by her praying downstairs in the living room. Usually, I would get up and go join her. She and Donna Ryan came to visit me once at my apartment in Harlem.

Dining Room/ Kitchen: heart, intent, motive, plans, passion, ambition. Song of Solomon 2:4 KJV, "He brought me to the banqueting house, and His banner over me is Love."

Clean, white laundry: covering, righteousness, spirit. Psalm 132: 9a KJV, "Let thy priests be clothed in righteousness."

Bedroom: rest, intimacy, privacy. Psalm 63:6 KJV, "When I remember thee upon my bed and meditate on thee in the night watches."

Psalm 77:6 AKJV, "I call to remembrance my song in the night. I will commune with mine own heart: and my spirit made diligent search."

Upstairs room: spiritual thought, prayer, spiritual service. Acts 10: 9b, 10b KJV, "Peter went up to the house top to pray... he fell into a trance."

Big smile: Psalm 45:7 KJV, "thou lovest righteousness and hatest wickedness: therefore God, thy God, hath anointed thee with the oil of gladness above thy fellows."

$186,000.00: Thousand = full stature, service, mature judgment. Ephesians 5:17 KJV, "Wherefore, be not unwise But, understanding what the will of the Lord is..."

Bobbie Jean Merck prophecy:

Sunday evening July 21st, 2002.

New Wine Christian Center

Wrightsville, Pa

"You are a seed planter Steven. God is using you in this area. Now hear me. Hear me, it is already beginning that you are going to have apostolic and prophetic anointing on praise and worship. As they seek the Apostle, they will begin to seek you. They will begin to seek you because you are a pattern laid down. People will cut their praise and worship by the pattern of praise and worship that is manifested through your leadership. 10 nations are waiting for you right now. It is in the anointing Steven. The anointing. Apostolic and prophetic.

Yes, and there will even be times when you will go and receive from them. And it will add to the treasury of God that is within you. Yes, here is your answer,

Steven. You are in the right place, for the right season. Steven, the Lord shows me you have given up the precious to obey God. And God says, that was an Ishmael for you. Your Isaac has come. Hallelujah!"

Pastor Qwest prophecy:

Sunday morning October 30, 2022

Victory City Church

Tyler, Texas

"Steven Sluder. There are promotions happening here. Promotions in the spirit. I have been sensing it and sensing it. And for no agenda concerning this ministry. Steven, the Lord is going to take you places you have never been before. There is an opening of doors. There were things that had to take place in your life spiritually before these doors would open. I hear the sound of creaking, creaking, creaking, opening. Opportunities to speak. Opportunities to share your testimony, opportunities to preach, to prophesy, to minister the Gospel. Opportunities, opportunities, opportunities. There are opportunities coming your way to advance the kingdom of God. There are promotions happening in this church in the spirit realm. Taking place for the righteous. Those who love what he loves. And hate what he hates. That has no ounce of compromise on the inside. There are promotions taking place in the mighty name of Jesus!"

116

Notes

Notes

Notes

Notes

A Final Word From The Author

I see the day

I see the day when we are spreading the knowledge of the glory of the Lord to them that are in darkness because we speak the language of faith. The language of Heaven.

I see the day when God is bringing many sons unto glory.

I see the day many people will rise above the world and exchange its lies for the Truth of God in them.

I see the day many precious fruits of the earth will learn who they are in Christ and take their place seated with Him in heavenly places far above the power of the enemy and every name that is named. Even the name of homosexuality.

I see the day they will learn the keys of authority, worship, prayer and living the lifestyle of an overcomer.

I see the day when many people walk in their homes and city streets with the doorposts of their minds covered in the blood of Jesus.

This is the day the prophet Isaiah spoke of in 60:1-2 "arise, shine, for the light has come. And the glory of the Lord has risen upon you.

Darkness shall cover the earth and dense darkness the people. But the Lord shall arise upon you and His glory shall be seen."

This is the day of much more exceeding glory. The dispensation of the Spirit shall be much more glorious.

This is the day His power and His glory will be seen in the sanctuary.

This is the day of harvest and rejoicing at His Word as one who finds great spoil.

This is the day God is bringing MANY SONS UNTO GLORY!